The World as Presence
El mundo como ser

Marcelo Morales

The World as Presence
El mundo como ser

Translated by Kristin Dykstra

The University of Alabama Press
Tuscaloosa

The University of Alabama Press
Tuscaloosa, Alabama 35487-0380
uapress.ua.edu

Typeface: FF Scala

Manufactured in the United States of America
Cover image: "Untitled," photograph by Alejandro González, 2016;
courtesy of Alejandro González (alejandrogonzalez-studio.com)
Cover design: Steve Miller
Book Design: Publications Unit, Department of English, Illinois
State University, Director: Steve Halle, Intern: Chantel Reeder

Cataloging-in-Publication data is available from the
Library of Congress.
ISBN: 978-0-8173-5884-6
E-ISBN: 978-0-8173-9085-3

Contents

Acknowledgments, Appreciations

We dedicate this book to the memory of Migdalia Hernández Delgado.

Because this is the first book by Morales to appear in English, a series of recognitions and publications (including some poems in earlier versions) were invaluable for moving the project along. We're grateful to the editors of *Tripwire, Circumference: Poetry in Translation,* and *MAKE: A Chicago Literary Magazine* for publishing excerpts. In the early stages of the Spanish-language composition, a short selection from the beginning of the manuscript appeared in Spanish only in *Mandorla: New Writing from the Americas.* Later excerpts in the Spanish appeared in the Cuban magazine *La Noria* as well as the anthology *The Cuban Team (Los once poetas cubanos).*

Very special thanks are due to the editors and staff of *Gulf Coast,* who created a new prize for literary translation in 2014. When excerpts from *The World as Presence* received the prize, it was a tremendous lift for us. Kristin Dykstra particularly thanks inaugural judge Jen Hofer for her attentive reading and precise remarks.

Sachie Hernández Machín, Brian Collier, Juliet Lynd, Daniel Borzutzky and Hank Lazer offered thoughtful responses to the manuscript in progress, as well as practical support. We also appreciate the dedication of the University of Alabama Press and are grateful for Steve Miller's work on the book's design.

Finally, Reina María Rodríguez made many of our conversations possible. Without her spirited support of artistic community over the years, the translation would not exist today.

Marcelo Morales Cintero and Kristin Dykstra

Unwinding the Present

> Direct writing finally for the unwindment
> for the alleviation of forms
> for the decongestion of images
> of which the brain-public square in these times is especially glutted
> —Henri Michaux, from "Movements"

In *El mundo como ser (The World as Presence)*, Marcelo Morales Cintero[1] tracks sensations giving form to worlds inside and outside of the self. His book explores existence, presence and change in the city of Havana.

Havana appears in fragments organized into a cinematic montage. Morales tells me that he sees the reality of the city in a "fairly peculiar" way, thanks in part to the fact that he traveled outside Havana numerous times from 1999 to 2014. Upon each return to his home, "the city is read in a different way."[2]

Reading the city of Havana, and Cuba as a whole, is an established literary practice that opens windows into many possible dimensions of experience. It is also an exercise popular in the international press, where curiosity about the island tends to lead rapidly, and more narrowly, to political topics. Are Cuba's difference, and its long opposition to the US government, signs of an alternative present and future? Are they nostalgic visions from the post-1959 past? How has Cuba changed or not changed since 1989? What does it mean for Cuba to enter a new century after the loss of strategic alliances once enabled by the Soviet Union? A constant parade of speculations imagining potential Cuban futures has played out for decades, alongside the sequential deaths of futurities that never came to be.

The composition of *The World as Presence* took place from early 2013 into early 2015. It is a period of personal change during which Morales's approach to writing poetry expanded. Meanwhile, on the community front, he witnessed dramatic new signs of change. While Morales previously wrote poetry more oriented toward an interior, visionary zone outside social history, the boundaries between personal and public spheres turn permeable in *The World as Presence*.

Here Morales uses poetry to track the imprints that change makes on the mind. His lines manifest as the "stippling" of presence in society— flecks and scratches of the *ser*, a term that can conjure one's presence, being, and existence. For the translation of that key word I chose "presence" due to the precision of its sound and association with a present moment in time, rather than the option of "being," which may at first seem to be the more obvious, literal choice. Marking the time of the present while exploring one's own presence becomes a way to test claims and limits for change.

When addressing this topic, "change," *The World as Presence* necessarily begins and ends *in medias res*. Any tale of change in Cuba feeds into a longer continuum of tellings. I will in fact argue that stories about change in Havana are master narratives, by which I mean repeating constructs, patterns that link the late twentieth century to the twenty-first because so many people participate in this activity. As in all compelling stories, the observations shared through narratives about change are tense, meaningful, because they are permeated with hope and anxiety.

Rewinding only to the late 1980s, Cubans and observers witnessed a series of transformations and uncertainties that called for interpretation: the end of the Soviet era, the intense economic and social crises of the 1990s, and the turn into the new century. Meanwhile, throughout the post-1959 period, narratives describing change have existed alongside a powerful counter-narrative of non-change, one imagining an island "frozen in time" after supposedly falling out of the timeline of the modern world (defined, in this case, as a capitalist present). In 2015, the foundation of that particular counter-narrative finally seemed to be cracking, while alternate perceptions of change went on multiplying. What future is becoming possible for the island now?

Whereas other tellings (especially in the popular media) can lean toward sensationalizing changes in Cuba, Morales pursues sensation. He uses the freedom of poetic genre and juxtaposition in order to track sensations across different dimensions of existence.

Morales concluded *The World as Presence* just after registering a double shock whose sonic boom is too expansive to fit into the field of writing. The magnitude of this change is partly perceptible in the motion of his poetic fragments. They cohere, then lift and part ways.

Sensations of Change

The first of the two major shocks Morales experienced in late 2014 was personal. During the time elapsed in this book's composition, he slowly lost a beloved aunt to her battle with cancer, a process that he registers here in subtle tones. Loss sounds through the rhythm of a chemotherapy drip, and its agonizing pull is signaled with the incremental replacement of one figure for love by another. The romantic beloved, a stock figure in poetic traditions, appears elsewhere in Morales's writing but gets displaced for a while in *The World as Presence* by the implied presence of the aunt. Love associated with the familial figure takes over as the hospital temporarily moves to the fore. When death comes, it is quiet.

Playing across a broader social plane throughout *The World as Presence* are vague changes driven by uncertainty and speculation. These flow through Havana streets to the muffled beat of reggeutón. Shortly after the death of Morales's aunt in late 2014 came an abrupt change to that feeling of change at hand.

Let's call it an abrupt evolution in the rhetoric of Cuban change, an evolution that did not come quietly at all. Just as Morales was writing the final pages of his manuscript in December 2014, the presidents of the United States and Cuba, Barack Obama and Raúl Castro, made a dual announcement about their intention to change their infamously oppositional governmental relations for the better. The uncertain energies of change vibrating in Havana compressed into a new form.

This bilingual edition pairs Morales's Spanish-language manuscript with a translation into English, which I undertook in conversation with the author from 2013 to early 2015 while he composed and revised the book. Following Morales, I composed and revised my English version of the manuscript sensing that shocks were affecting the evolution of his poems before I had ways to describe what was happening.

Urban Backdrop: Vedado District

Morales's travels around and outside Cuba play into his particular way of reading and writing Havana. For a reader unfamiliar with the city's landmarks flitting through the fabric of the book, it's helpful to start by noting that much of *The World as Presence* registers sensation from a home base in Vedado, a district within Havana.

The poems do not attempt to "document" Vedado or the larger city of Havana in an overt fashion, and they make no claims to perform anthropology. Instead the contours of the city meld into their lines, the gaps between words, and the rhythms of their articulation.

The prose poems of *The World as Presence* dialogue with a tradition that scholars have tended to discuss more in terms of prose, particularly fiction. "Throughout the history of Cuban literature," observes Rafael Rojas, "there have been narrative strategies for dealing with the city where the writer has presented himself as the city's reader in times of symbolic mutation."[3] The almost manic nature of storytelling that attempts to decode change in Cuba—in the international media as well as island literature—proffers contemporary examples of the pattern Rojas has identified. *The World as Presence* complicates this mission by placing the city's reader in his own state of mutation. His refusal to "stay in place" and limit the focus of his perceptions actually works well with the form of the book. The white spaces of poetry are generous. The contemplative pace, lack of organic connectivity between its fragments, and changes in speed and scope of perception all allow the speaker to resist foreclosing on interpretations. The poetic self remains open to the fullness of sensation, allowing for freedom and patience while witnessing change.

Whether the act of "reading the city" foregrounds poetry or politics, words or politicians or buildings, an attempt to understand change in the Havana area takes some aspect of the city's long history into account. I offer brief contextual notes here for readers unfamiliar with subtle urban landmarks constituting a backdrop to poetic perception.

Havana did not initially appear destined for a starring symbolic role in literature. Joseph Scarpaci, Roberto Segre and Mario Coyula (authors of various important studies of architecture and urban life in Havana) assert that the city "was never characterized in the sixteenth to eighteenth centuries as a city of great splendor."[4] As the sugar industry grew, however, Havana developed into a complex urban terrain now famous for its diversity of architectural forms and lifeways.

Morales's own district of Vedado first began to take form as a new influx of sugar wealth in the late eighteenth and nineteenth centuries propelled expansion of Havana's neighborhoods, which would eventually diversify. He presently lives on Calle Línea, or Línea Street, which mostly lies about five blocks in from the ocean and runs roughly parallel to Havana's famous seaside boulevard known as the Malecón. The street also "marks the first separation between the coastal level and the first prominent escarpment," as the city's curving landmass slowly rises away from the water (Scarpaci et al 8).

Various stages of development inform urban landmarks and road-ways that pulse through *The World as Presence*. In the 19th century Vedado was considered part of the "New" Havana expansion known in part for luxurious building style and boulevard design. A feature of this legacy still visible today is the use of columns on buildings set back from streets. Another is the use of the *parterre*, or tree-lined corridor dividing some roads from their sidewalk, as seen on Paseo, another major boulevard in the area. Vedado's often patrician look disguises a mixture of social classes living in the district, as in the early example of tenement homes nestled behind elegant façades (Scarpaci et al 56).

The arrival of US power and capital in the twentieth century forwarded urban design in ways that symbolized change in their moment. The road system linking Vedado to neighboring districts was soon expanded. By the 1930s the influential French landscape designer Forestier treated the seaside boulevard, the Malecón, as a key element in the "water edge," which he saw as an exterior border and visual introduction to the city. Forestier argued for design further enhancing the seaside connections between Vedado's waterfront and neighboring areas, as well as expansion of natural areas. Beginning in the late 1940s, Vedado's shopping center at La Rampa became another symbol of progress for twentieth-century Habaneros. Movie theaters, offices, cafeterias and other businesses arose along this sloped area.

The 1950s expanded on these changes with high-rise architecture, a feature highlighted in this edition with the author portrait of Marcelo Morales. This image was taken by his close friend, Alejandro González. González first attracted national attention with a 1999 photographic series exploring the relation between the city and a series of people who inhabit it, entitled "Quién" ("Who"). His ongoing interest in connecting portraiture to place hints at creative affinities with Morales, as well as emphasizing Vedado's role as a backdrop.[5]

As a series of hotels characterized by modern and high-rise styling appeared in Vedado near La Rampa in the 1950s, they helped to turn Vedado into "the premiere tourist district of Havana," and today they are still landmarks for navigating the city. The Habana Riviera, the Hilton (now the Habana Libre), and the Capri all figure amongst these constructions (Scarpaci et al 121–2). High-rise apartments also added to Vedado's verticality. Meanwhile, visitors and investors could rub shoulders with

Havana's upper class in country clubs, another urban structure expressing influences of the moment. American clubs joined earlier upper-crust social societies dotting Vedado. The University of Havana offered another sort of gathering space, and not only as an institution of higher education. It became a site of intervention in public debate, particularly during the rising tensions of the 1950s: "Its central location just a few blocks from the heart of the Vedado tourist district served to disseminate news reports of violent conflicts between students and police" (Scarpaci et al 96). These institutions and innovations, in tandem with the labors of organized crime families who aimed to make the city a cornerstone in their Miami/Vegas/Havana tourism-and-gambling triad, all represented dominant forces influencing the shape of Havana prior to 1959.

After the Revolution time did not actually skid to a stop, no matter how insistently this idea has been proclaimed. A more egalitarian social space was envisioned for Vedado, as new leaders deliberately rejected earlier projects focused on moneyed privacy. For example, a green space around the Coppelia ice cream parlor at L and 23rd Streets "serves as a public space, town square, and point of encounter for what used to be commonly referred to as the revolution's *hombre integrado* [new, integrated person]" (Scarpaci et al 305). The revolutionary government famously curtailed tourism and nationalized hotels, projecting not only the construction of a "new" social space but a new Cuban person to boot.

Vedado today boasts substantial business and medical services along with its residential blocks, due in part to expansions of services under the revolutionary government. However, it's also marked by the shortages and uncertainties of the immediate post-Soviet moment, then the turn into the twenty-first century, when new contrasts in wealth are becoming visible as private business reemerges. Contemporary literature from Cuba offers many works that revisit the rhetoric of everyday life in the post-1989 era, an era of transition that has included severe economic crisis, a scramble for new global allies as the former Soviet support system dropped away, and a wealth of speculation about the new order still to be fully understood in the twenty-first century. Tourism is making an aggressive return to the streets of Vedado, probably for the better as well as the worse, which constitutes one of many changes that Morales registers in the cinematic fragments comprising *The World as Presence*.

Vedado, then, is never static—and neither is the person who perceives it. Whereas stillness and interior meditations claim space in many of Morales's poems, the speaker is just as often out in the city, in motion. His figure, its gaze, moves down roads on foot or in a car, goes in and out of buildings. In one poem he drives through the second of two tunnels built in the 1950s, one that connected the Malecón to Quinta Avenida, or Fifth Avenue, in 1959. In others, a sense of jostling over urban space emerges from a discomfort framed in gendered terms—with other males in the street, with anonymous women in an anonymous bar, a scene that originated from a bar atop the tall FOCSA building in Vedado.

In, Out, Around

Morales complicates the grounds of the book with fragmented memories from his physical travel in and around the greater Havana area, in other parts of Cuba, and abroad.

In older sections of the city readers see him move down the Prado, passing famous landmarks such as the theater housing the National Ballet; and down Galiano, a street dividing Old Havana from Central Havana. A poem communicating notable tension early in the book refers to his participation in a poetry festival in the eastern housing community of Alamar. While I will highlight the fact that this important moment happened in a different, outlying area of Havana, the significant memory for Morales centers on the act of reading aloud in front of the Alamar audience. There he first shared work in progress with a political content new to his writing.

Additional urban markers scatter in relation to Morales's daily itineraries. He drives through the city in the family's aging Lada sedan, giving him driver's-side views of locations such as the Malecón. In brief frames we see the Quinta Avenida road and tunnel, which take vehicles off toward the western side of the city, as well as a piece of highway near Havana that locals call "las ocho vías" (the eight lanes).

Brief recollections of family homes enter these poems, melding fragments of the past into the urban present. Morales recalls his parents' apartment in the Havana neighborhood of La Timba, and he departs the city entirely in a memory of his grandfather's home in the town of Rodas, in Cienfuegos Province.

Flashes of travel to yet more distant places further expand and shift the time and place of the book. Once, Morales recalls, he arrived at a hill overlooking the US Naval Base at Guantanamo; on that night, perhaps in 2012, a place that he had only known as an abstract idea became real to him through the light it sent up. There are also momentary glimpses from his visits to the Jewish quarter in Rome in 2001, to Berlin in 2013, and to the border separating France from Spain in the Pyrenees at an unspecified moment. Significant factors leading to his periodic travels outside the island have included an extended stay in Italy for university study, visits to family members who live and work in other parts of Latin America, and a variety of cultural invitations to present his writing abroad.

These brief spatterings from other places and times fold into the stippling motions of the poems. They enable Morales to create idiosyncratic views of Vedado, of Havana, and even of Cuba, cutting across shared community experiences with signs of individual perception.

New Generations / New Possibilities

The World as Presence showcases a voice from a particular generation, another register carrying both community and individual resonance. Morales was born in Cuba in 1977. He is an established, prizewinning writer. Simultaneously he is "younger" in comparison to most of the island poets known worldwide to date, many of whom were born prior to the 1959 Revolution. His first book of poetry appeared in Cuba in 1997, when he was twenty years old.

Morales developed his writing in various relationships to prose. This includes material that would be easily classified in narrative genres, such as a novel. More significant to date, however, is his prose poetry, which exploits intersections between genres. Most often delivered in sparing and contemplative lines, his book-length works make use of abrupt contrast, allowing a poem to suddenly expand in length. The tension between short and longer lines allows Morales to shift from disconnection into pulsing syntheses, permitting musicality and speed that he resists in the pages foregrounding more white space.

Dedicated to the slow development of his book projects, Morales has earned many of his awards for segments of larger works in progress. For example, excerpts that later came together to form his poetry collection *El mundo como objeto* won the 2004 poetry prize from *La Gaceta de Cuba*, as well as an honorable mention for the national Julián del Casal prize and a coveted finalist position in the international Casa de las Américas competition. The first edition of the complete book appeared in 2006 from Isla Negra Editores, winning an award from the Puerto Rican PEN Club, and a second edition followed in Cuba a year later.

Morales is also the author of the poetry collections *Cinema* (1997, Pinos Nuevos prize), *El círculo mágico* (2007), and *Materia* (winner of the 2008 Julián del Casal prize), among others. His novel *La espiral* appeared in 2006. Morales edited and introduced *Como un huésped de la noche* (2010), an anthology of work by Roberto Branly, a Cuban predecessor who also explored both prose and poetry.[6]

As his author's note opening *The World as Presence* asserts, Morales situates his books of prose poetry as part of a continuum. He described his metaphors for beauty in poetry to me during the translation process. These pursue an elegance that is meticulously direct, sheared off, and pared down. His collections display a desire to tap the most essential features of life, trace its contours and explore the range and complexity of human possibility within everyday life.

In search of his own contours, the speaker seeks out the edgings of death. The emotional intensities of his quest alternate with numbness. That alternation may be a rhythm essential for survival, but the speaker wages war on his moments of numbness anyway, determined to make room for love. Love allows the self to emerge from isolation in its discovery of the beloved, an *other* presence, and to express hope.

Morales read a great deal of international literature while developing his own distinct voice. As a younger writer interested in prose poetry and the crafting of a sentence, he was attracted to French writers. One is François de la Rochefoucauld, particularly his maxims, which makes sense for a writer so interested in the power of short, philosophically resonant lines. "The Drunken Boat," by Arthur Rimbaud (1854–1891), has periodically seduced Morales with its ecstatic, visionary qualities. I would place even more emphasis on Henri Michaux (1899–1984), whose search for a poetic zone demonstrates great complexity of thought and form. Michaux influenced Morales in his abandonment of traditional lyric forms. While Michaux drops many conventions and allows poetry to wander into paragraphs of prose, he is still known for projecting musicality and inventiveness.

Morales eventually moved in other aesthetic directions and minimizes direct French influence in his discussions of the writing from the current decade. Michaux, for example, had a more obvious influence on

Morales's 2007 collection *El círculo mágico* (*The Circle's Spell*) than on the current book. At the same time I see indirect continuities worked into the handling of the poems. In his fragmented pieces Morales retains a sense of commitment to strangeness and alienation, as well as the sense of hostility often running through the environment around the speaker that animates much of Michaux's work. These features are counter-balanced and enhanced in Morales's writings by intense curiosity about the great spaces, even an infinite space, to be found within the self.

Another writer who carried more weight earlier in Morales's career is Antonin Artaud, yet Artaud leaves an undeniable mark on *The World as Presence*: his imagery of stippling is central to the book's aesthetic strategy. A brief quotation from Artaud appearing as the epigraph to poem 34 makes that link explicit. Just as important are the complete poems 34 and 37, two of the longest pieces in the book. These refer to stipplings of perception while dramatizing the motions of the mind.

The greatest difference between *The World as Presence* and the earlier collections appears in Morales's increasing range. He now draws not only on conversations with other writers but on a widening array of resources for creating literature. The writers whom he finds to be most present in this book are often named openly in epigraphs or the body of a poem: José Alvarez Baragaño, José Lezama Lima, Virgilio Piñera, Joseph Brodsky, Tomas Transtömer, E.E. Cummings, Jack Spicer (whose writing Morales first saw via a translation by David Menéndez Álvarez, published in *Mandorla* 14), Gottfried Benn, Philip Larkin, and Charles Simic. Just as significant are a series of resources that Morales describes as "less poetic and more audiovisual, cinematographic." In this category he lists "reality, the bad kind of regguetón, newspapers, propaganda posters" and the arenas of visual art, television, and history books. "Now I try to use it all," he concludes.

Using everything has brought a new maturity to his poetry. Morales's earlier books are characterized by a feel of cleanliness: poetry acts as a defense of interiority, usually keeping the community at bay. Where the poetry's serenity gets ruffled, tension tends to form through interactions with a poetic beloved and/or confrontations with the boundary-negating power of death. Whereas the opening page of *The World as Presence* continues in this meditative pattern, it rapidly becomes clear that the speaker no longer succeeds at guarding his interior spaces so thoroughly from contamination from the urban life all around him . . . and perhaps he has given up the effort.

It is in the permeation of Morales's former poetic boundaries where I find the most interesting moments of the new book. He allows battles between internal and external realities to surface after many years of pushing them below the reader's lines of sight. For this reason, I return to the relation between self and society to conclude these introductory remarks.

Like the theme of love, the public life of Cuba threads through *The World as Presence* in a different way than in Morales's earlier books. Morales touches on shifts and contradictions in Cuba's economy and society under the island's post-Fidel leadership. He also communicates some ambivalence about how "new" that leadership may be, since Raúl Castro is not only of the same generation and family as his brother, but of the same party. Still his gradual and highly planned openings toward small-scale capitalism have begun to alter daily life for Havana residents, as has an atmosphere of general expectation and anxiety.

It is by no means clear what this much-hyped and much-debated state of transition will become in the long term. In fact, times and spaces go on multiplying, creating what Rojas describes as "a ritualized chaos" in writing from Cuba at the turn of the twenty-first century: "From the beginning of the 1990s, people in Havana felt nostalgias for all Havanas, including nostalgias for the most immediate past, the one just before `the crisis.' However, since Fidel Castro's convalescence in the summer of 2006 or, more precisely, since the transfer of power in 2008 the future is being lived alongside every imaginable past and present" (Rojas 123). As residents "begin to lose their sense of historical orientation," Rojas observes, their disorientation finds expression in literature in the merging of time frames: "The temporality of the island begins to function in a synchronic sense instead of a diachronic one" (129). Distinct times, real and imaginary, compress into the present rather than remaining clearly distinguished. *The World as Presence* demonstrates this trait, and as poems remarking on politicians show, Morales is also taking a turn toward reading Havana "in terms of power dynamics" while presenting those observations from the perspective of someone who lacks power and control, another tendency noted by Rojas in contemporary Cuban prose (128–9).

Local and global patterns of obsessive attention to change in Cuba, coupled with a slowness experienced by many islanders as an everyday limbo, took a marked turn with the famous dual announcements of December 2014 when Obama stated his desire to normalize relations between the United States and Cuba, and Raúl Castro delivered a public partner statement to his nation. While they induced an instant media frenzy around the idea of change, these announcements did not immediately end the United States economic embargo of Cuba, an institution that had a profound impact on both nations for more than half a century. In this climate, how do you map the new shapes and risks of public discourse? Of literary expression that divulges private thought alongside public sights?

Where Morales melds memories into his perceptions of the present, it is particularly important to recognize that his poems signal tension between speaking in unison and speaking alone. Lines from political slogans and famous poetry taught in Cuban schools return from Morales's childhood, another generational marker and perhaps, to follow Rojas's logic, an expression of nostalgia for what felt like a more stable time.

This tension creates a challenge for the translator: how to draw attention to essential context that many readers will not have experienced. In the book as a whole, I've made little expansion within the poems to communicate social or historical contexts. Instead Morales and I decided to place clarifications in a collaboratively written "Notes on the Poems" section at the end, which emphasizes Morales's own memories and associations; as well as including some material here in the introduction. But because a sense of unison is such an important touchstone of both aesthetics and social relations in *The World as Presence*, I inserted one phrase asserting unison within Poem 37. The mood of the original poem relies on conjuring a generation's memory of being raised to recite certain lines together, in support of a collective vision.

While he refers to this instruction in school, Morales's own poetry is not didactic. It doesn't explain to the reader *how* these moments from the past are entering the present—perhaps because his meditations are truly meditations, not platform statements. Instead *The World as Presence* tracks a single person's process of crossing borders between the unison of childhood and the many dividing lines cutting through his adult present.

Certain fragments of *The World as Presence* suggest a frustrated desire to locate a viable political perspective, which brings an additional layer of emotional and civic risk into the poems. The most complicated element of this desire is that the speaker does not position himself as a dissident, although some poems indicate a critical view of the status quo in Cuba. They express distance from official rhetoric in a way characteristic of many citizens confronting the uncertainties of the twenty-first century. Many younger Cubans have learned their regional history and understand the importance of anti-imperialist political positions, yet they are wary of power's centralizations on the left as well as the right.

The World as Presence, resisting platforms, hints instead at the ongoing proliferation of necessary questions. How much of one's interior and exterior realities will be determined by politicians, whom Morales eventually sets off from everyone else as the "alphas" with their own space? Morales has remarked on his inability to identify with any current party today, which leaves him in limbo, an outsider to power. This is not to say he doesn't have political desires. Outside the context of this book, he sketched for me the possible future emergence of a left democratic party that could value ecological health, public civility, education, democracy, and independence. But to date political pluralism has been constrained by numerous factors.

The resulting questions erupt into poetry, where they become part of its directness—a personal unwinding of the twisted skeins of public speech, and a re-twisting of lines into more private threads.

Even at its most direct, the poetry makes no claims about a future self. The awareness of mortality running throughout *The World as Presence* makes it possible to recognize both self and city as perpetually evaporating worlds. Morales ends with a simple present-tense assertion: "I am alive."

Kristin Dykstra

Notes

Epigraph. Translated by Bernard Bador and Clayton Eshleman. *The Volta* 5 (May 2012, "They Will Sew the Blue Sail"). Digital: http://www.thevolta.org/twstbs-poem15-hmichaux. html.

1. In keeping with Hispanic usages, the author has two last names: Morales and Cintero. The author follows a common practice of treating the first surname, passed down from the father's family, as his default surname. It is the one most comparable to a last name as used in English. I give both surnames to open the introduction because two family names can appear in Spanish-language formal and legal situations; for this reason his

mother's surname, Cintero, has appeared in connection with some of the author's literary publications.

2. Morales and I were able to discuss earlier versions of the manuscript in person in 2013 and again in early 2014. Our conversations after that point, such as the one from 29 September 2015 that I'm citing here, took place primarily over email. I cite this same message later in the introduction, where Morales talks about his expanded sense of resources for writing.

3. "The Illegible City: Havana After the Messiah." Tr. Eric Felipe-Barkin. In *Havana Beyond the Ruins: Cultural Mappings after 1989*, ed. Anke Birkenmaier and Esther Whitfield, 2011. 119–34.

4. *Havana: Two Faces of the Antillean Metropolis*. 2nd ed. Chapel Hill and London: The University of North Carolina Press, 2002. 21.

5. For an overview of González's photography, see "Alejandro González: Chronicling a City Called Home" by Ricardo Alberto Pérez, translated to English for *Cuba Absolutely* (January 2013). Digital: http://www.cubaabsolutely.com/Culture/article_photography.php?id=Alejandro-Gonzalez-Chronicling-a-city-called-home.

6. Morales has a familial relation to Branly, who married his aunt Migdalia Hernández—the same aunt who is also important to this collection in her own right. Branly passed away when Morales was only three years old. However, his legacy survives. Today Morales lives in the same apartment that Branly once shared with his aunt. He inherited Branly's personal library, one of many ways in which the older writer profoundly affected Morales's relationship to literature.

The World as Presence
El mundo como ser

Photograph of Marcelo Morales © Alejandro González, 2016

Nota del autor

Este libro empieza como un diálogo, luego de muchos años, con uno de mis primeros libros de poesía, *El mundo como objeto*, 2004. *El mundo como objeto* partía de un verso de Lautréamont en el que se refería al mundo como "ese gran objeto exterior". En el transcurso de su escritura, fue ocurriendo en mi país, un cambio de poder político que se fue infiltrando en él. El diálogo con una realidad interior y exterior viva, es su hilo conductor.

Author's Note

This book begins as a conversation, after many years, with one of my first poetry collections, *El mundo como objeto* (*The World as Object*, 2004). *El mundo como objeto* departs from a line by Lautréamont in which he refers to the world as "that great exterior object." In the course of its composition, something was happening in my country. A change in political power began to infiltrate the writing. The dialogue between an interior reality and a living exterior is its central thread.

1

Leía un poema de Gottfried Benn, hablaba de un cadáver sobre una mesa de disección, describía la manera en que tocaba el cerebro, la manera en que extraía su lengua y la ponía en un recipiente con agua "like flowers".

Oí a una multitud gritando atrás por la ventana, una multitud gritando libertad.

Detrás iba una turba gritando cosas violentas.

Libertad, libertad.

Dejé los órganos en el búcaro, agarré mi cámara, me puse las botas sin medias y fui al edificio de prisiones.

Cuando llegué no vi ya a nadie, un guardia joven me dijo que por favor tomara la calle, sólo por hoy, me dijo.

Yo pensaba en los órganos de Gottfried.

Sentí emoción por la palabra libertad, creo que eran Las Damas, regresé a la casa, mientras subía las escaleras pensé, tu problema no es la cobardía, tu problema es la indiferencia

1

I was reading a poem by Gottfried Benn, it talked about a cadaver on a dissection table, describing the way he touched its cerebellum, the way he extracted the tongue and placed it, "como flores," into a receptacle with water.

Through the back window I heard a crowd shouting, a crowd shouting freedom.

Behind it a mob shouting violent things.

Freedom, freedom.

I left the organs in the jar, grabbed my camera, threw on my boots without socks and went out toward the prison bureau.

When I arrived I didn't see anyone, a young guard told me to please walk in the street, just for today, he said.

I thought about Gottfried's organs.

I was struck by hearing the word freedom, I think it was a protest by the Ladies, I returned to my house, as I was climbing the stairs I thought, your problem isn't cowardice, your problem is indifference.

2

Estaba en ese bar de lesbianas, una cerveza en mis manos. Lo supe, no tengo alma, no existe el alma. Las lesbianas no me querían ahí. Caminé por la línea de la barra. La cerveza no era amarilla any more. El mundo no es objeto, es un ser, y está vivo.

2

I was in that lesbian bar, a beer in my hands. I realized I have no soul, the soul doesn't exist. The lesbians didn't want me there. I walked along the line of the bar. The beer wasn't yellow any more. The world is not an object, it's a presence, and it's alive.

3

Frente a mi cerveza, yo pude ver sus cerebros, el verdadero ser. No tengo alma, me dije, tengo cerebro. Frente a la computadora chateamos, los amigos por el mundo. Deberíamos fundar el partido apolítico. Éramos los hijos de La Revolución, pero también de la dictadura. Habíamos perdido de vista el socialismo, pensando que el socialismo era Fidel. Habíamos perdido de vista la igualdad, pensando que igualdad era él.

3

Face to my beer I could see its cerebellum, the real presence. I don't have a soul, I said to myself, I have a cerebellum. Face to the computer we chat, friends around the world. We should found the apolitical party. We were the children of the Revolution but also of the dictatorship. We had lost sight of socialism, thinking that socialism was Fidel. We had lost sight of equality, thinking that equality was him.

4

Ayer mientras leía un poema político me tembló la mano. Sentí la presión del poder, mi miedo al poder. Ayer, mientras leía, temblé, como la primera vez. Cuando salí, me encontré en un bar con mis amigos, hablé de todo sin decirles nada. Oscar gritaba borracho, la otra pedía tequila. Aunque nos quedamos, hace tiempo que nos fuimos.

4

Yesterday while I was reading a political poem my hand shook. I felt the weight of power, my fear of power. Yesterday as I was reading I shook, just like the first time. When I left I met friends in a bar, talked about everything while telling them nothing. Oscar was drunk and shouting, someone else ordered tequila. Even though we stay here, we left a long time ago.

5

Yo supe a cada instante de la fugacidad de la vida, por eso a cada instante sufrí lo que no debía, por eso también a cada instante disfruté.

Ayer, mientras regaba las matas pensé: La vida se trata de perder, de ganar, pero de perder, uno pierde al menos, un día cada día. La vida está hecha de los seres, el ancla con el mundo es el ser, el mundo como un ser, como los seres.

5

At one time I could feel the fugacity of life in every instant, which is why I suffered every instant as I should not have, which is why I enjoyed every one of them.

Yesterday while watering plants I thought: life is about loss, about gain, but about loss; we lose at least one day every day. Life is made of presences, the anchor to the world is presence, the world as presence, as presences.

6

Fuimos a ver la casa de mi bisabuelo, una casa de columnas fuertes, a las que les caía a tiros mentando a Machado.

Recordaba a uno de los hermanos de mi abuelo recostado en una silla echándose aire con una penca. No quedaba nada ahí, de la casa, de los negocios, nada.

Los mundos desaparecen, me dijo mi padre en casa de mi abuela, es un mundo que desapareció, como desaparecerá este.

Esquinas que solo existen en la mente. Objetos. Hay cosas que guardan lo más bello de nosotros, amar, es encontrarse, dicen.

6

We went to see my great-grandfather's house, a house with strong columns. He shot at them, calling Machado's name.

I remembered one of my grandfather's brothers who rested in a chair, fanning himself. Nothing was left there, nothing of the house, the businesses, nothing.

Worlds disappear, my father told me at my grandmother's house, that world disappeared, like this one will disappear.

Street corners existing only in the mind. Objects. There are things that protect the most beautiful part of us, to love is to find yourself, they say.

7

El mundo no había cambiado pero yo sí. Un día después de tu muerte, mientras hablábamos de ti, cayó un lucero, un meteorito, creo. Algo bajó echando chispas del cielo. Luego fuimos a comprar cerveza, yo ponía las monedas sobre el cristal del mostrador. La muerte, cuando es literatura, es profunda, pensé, cuando es real, increíble.

7

The world had not changed but I did. One day after your death, while we
were talking about you, a star streaked past, a meteorite I guess. Some-
thing fell, shooting sparks from the sky. Then we went out to buy beer,
I put coins on the glass top of the display case. When death is literature
it's profound, I thought, when death is real it's incredible.

8

Es poco lo que no cae en el vacío del pasado, la habilidad de pensar es idéntica, como habilidad, a cualquiera. Constante relación del ser con la nada. La relación del vacío. Abrí un osario y vi los huesos, una cajita donde las tibias estaban al lado del cráneo. Un saco gris. Aunque la muerte se confunda con la nada no son lo mismo. Aunque la vida se confunda con el ser, tampoco.

8

There is little that does not disappear into the past. The ability to think,
as abilities go, is just like any other. Constant relation between being
and nothingness. The relation to the void. I opened an ossuary and saw
the bones, a little box where tibias rested next to the skull. A gray blazer.
Though death may get confused with nothingness they're not the same.
Though life may get confused with presence, they're not the same either.

9

Los místicos hablan del Vacío como una abstracción. Yo hablo del vacío como un hecho. Atravieso la miseria. Habana, Carlos Tercero, piedra sucia. El sonido del hambre no está en el estómago. El sonido del hambre está en la mente. Algunos seres se definen por los órganos que los rigen. Aparatos intestinales. En mi casa, paredes sin pintar. En la televisión el gran líder. Camino hacia la sala. Todo el que prohíbe, prohíbe por poder, pienso. Las imposiciones no tienen ideología que las sustenten. Es importante que lo sepan, esto que soy, soy yo, no ustedes. Es importante que sepan. El asno camina siempre en la montaña. El asno, está siempre a un paso del abismo.

9

The mystics talk about the Void as an abstraction. I talk about the void as a fact. I move through decay. Havana, Carlos Tercero Street, grimy stone. Hunger makes a sound that doesn't come from the stomach. The sound of hunger is in the mind. Some beings are defined by organs that govern them. Intestinal systems. Inside my house: walls with no paint. On televisions the great leader. I walk toward the living room. Everything prohibited is prohibited through power, I think. The impositions have no ideology supporting them. It's important for you all to know: this thing that I am is me, not you. It's important for you all to know. The donkey always walks along the mountainside. The donkey, it's always one step from the abyss.

10

El arte como pensamiento, la conciencia interna de las cosas. Dos mone-
das en el suelo, me levanto, pongo mis pies en la loza. In the name of
revolution, Habana, Carlos Tercero, lluvia, in the name of. Un travesti
con zapatos amarillos, cincuenta años de gobierno in the name. Paredes
blancas entrando en mis sentidos, Brigadas de Respuesta in the name, el
amor in the name. Habana- Vedado, Malecón buscando Línea. Cuando
dicen revolución dicen en verdad conservación. La libertad es algo de
lo que los poderes hablan, la libertad es algo que el poder consiente, la
libertad es cosa de poder. Toda esta gente tiene una vida, una sola vida,
el arte, la política, es, como el excremento, tiene la calidad de lo que se
come.

10

Art as thought, the internal awareness of things. Two coins on the floor,
I get up, put my feet down on cold tile. *In the name of the revolution,*
Havana, Carlos Tercero, rain, *in the name of.* A transvestite with yellow
shoes, fifty years of government *in the name.* White walls pervading
my senses, Response Brigades *in the name,* love *in the name.* Havana:
Vedado, the Malecón running along the sea in search of Línea Street.
When they say revolution they really mean conservation. Freedom is
something of which the powers speak, freedom is something to which
power consents, freedom is a thing of power. All these people have a
life, just one life, art, politics, being of, like excrement, having, the same
quality as what you eat.

11

Hace años que no escribo, me digo. En la calle, a mi lado, un taxi
amarillo.

En el horizonte el sol se mueve como un huevo. El fin de la historia,
paso el túnel, rayas de separación, el sol, una yema violácea. Nada por lo
cual morir. El fin de la historia, digo. Cansancio. Bandada de yanquis,
zapatos blancos, medias blancas, tenis, todo blanco, the cuban marrra-
cas, the cuban artist. The Cubans. El centro de la fruta es el hueso, leí.
El centro de mí. Entro a un bar, ahora todo es privado, gente cool, gente
rica, ahora todo es privado, diseño, ahora todo es diseño. Hay muchas
maneras de suicidarse, me dicen. Cerrar los ojos es una. Salgo del bar,
el sol me abre la frente, me abre la frente lo real. Después de mirarlo por
un rato, la compañía violácea. Necesidad terrible de un poema, necesi-
dad de arte.

Escuchar tu voz en soledad, la voz de tu espíritu, hay maneras de no
estar, de anularse, me dicen, cerrar los ojos es una, creo, cierro los ojos,
la masa violácea flotando en mi retina. Una o, un cero violeta, un círculo
trazado por una realidad violenta. No podrán decir que yo acepté el
abuso. No podrán decir: La raíz de su amor dejó de luchar en la frontera.
No podrán decir, que yo acepté esta nada.

11

I haven't written for years, I say to myself. In the street next to me, a yellow taxi.

On the horizon the sun wobbles like an egg. The end of history, I pass the tunnel, dividing lines, the sun, a violet-colored yolk. Nothing for which to die. End of story, I say. Exhaustion. A gang of Yankees, white shoes, white socks, sneakers, everything white, *the Cuban mahh-racas, the Cuban artist. The Cubans.* The center of the fruit is the pit. I read that. The center of me. I go into a bar, now everything is private, cool people, rich people, now everything is private, designed, now design is everything. There are a lot of ways to kill yourself, they tell me. Closing your eyes is one of them. I leave the bar, the sun strikes my forehead, reality strikes my forehead. After looking at it for a while, violet accompaniment. Terrible need for a poem, need for art.

Listening to your voice in solitude, your spirit's voice, there are ways to not be there, to void yourself, they say, closing your eyes is one way, I think, I close my eyes, the violet mass floating in my retina. A letter "o," a violet zero, a circle drawn by a violent reality. They won't be able to say that I consented to the abuse. Won't be able to say: The source of his love gave out at the end of an era. Won't be able to say I consented to this nothingness.

12

Tres canas en el mentón.
Yo creí que el mundo hablaría todo el tiempo de mi amor,
que el futuro estaba lleno de mi amor.

Da Vinci decía que el ser no podía caer en la nada.
Si un amor como el que yo sentí pudo caer en la nada,
entonces mi vida podría también.
Si un amor puede caer en la nada, cualquier cosa puede.

12

Three gray hairs on my chin.
I believed that the world would always be talking about my love,
that the future was filled with my love.

Da Vinci used to say that being couldn't collapse into nothingness.
If a love like the one I felt could collapse into nothingness,
then so could my life.
If love can collapse into nothingness, anything can.

13

En el mojado cuenco de la boca,
me plantaste la voz
que te llamaba a gritos.
—Joseph Brodsky

Yo sé que te pusiste linda para mí, la sombra azul en tus ojos.

Tú creaste en mí este amor, para que este amor de ti necesitara.

Ya ves, encendiste mi vida para dejarla girando,

como un planeta loco, la sombra de tus ojos, la sombra azul.

Yo sé que te pusiste linda para mí, así se enciende algo,

así, luego de encendido, se abandona.

13

It was you [. . .]
who laid in my raw cavern
a voice calling you back.
—Joseph Brodsky

I know you made yourself lovely for me, the blue shadow in your eyes.

You created this love inside me, so this love would have need of you.

You see you ignited my life to set it spinning,

like a crazed planet, the shadow from your eyes, blue shadow.

I know you made yourself lovely for me, that's how something ignites,

how once ignited it abandons itself.

14

Y te buscaba como una serpiente en el fango como una rata en la basura
te buscaba, como un hambriento, los poetas me decían no hables de
eso, de eso no se habla, te buscaba en esas caras, en los años te buscaba,
entre las calles te buscaba, a veces, frente a frente, el corazón, se iba
hacia ella como la masa en el espacio, y daba un golpe y daba otro, como
si el imán lo llamara, como una rata en la basura, como una serpiente en
el fango, te buscaba.

14

And I sought you out like a snake in mud, like a rat in trash sought you, like one starving, the poets told me don't talk about that, people don't talk about that, I sought you out in those faces, in those years sought you out, among streets sought you out, sometimes, face to face, my heart, it would move toward her like mass in space, and it gave one thump and gave another, as if the attraction were calling it, like a rat in trash, like a snake in mud, sought you out.

15

Puedo percibir sucesos de otros mundos
en lo más profundo y oculto de mi mente
y en la mente de los demás
—Jim Morrison

Berlín, The Mauer. Lo que el sonido de un vaso al caer te comunica.
Crustáceos muertos en el congelador.
Puedo percibir mi muerte en mi mente y en la muerte de los otros.
Lo que el sonido de un vaso al caer te comunica.
Puedo sentir el muro en mi mente y en la mente de los otros.

15

> I can perceive events on other worlds,
> in my deepest inner mind,
> & in the minds of others
> —Jim Morrison

Berlin, *The Mauer*. What the sound of a falling glass communicates to you.
Dead crustaceans in the freezer.
I can perceive my death in my mind and in the deaths of the others.
What the sound of a falling glass communicates to you.
I can feel the wall in my mind and in the minds of the others.

16

El vacío entra como el timbre en una casa
—José Lezama Lima

Como un despertador entra la muerte
—J. A. Baragaño

Habana, huevones sentados en los muros, huevones en las esquinas, el vendedor - el chulo - el dient'é oro, peste a meao en los portales, la vieja comunista - la vieja gusana, el bloguero narciso, el comunista cretino, el indiferente, gente chea. Alemanes gordos - mulaticas flacas, los ojos en mis ojos, alemanes gordos - mulaticas, Lada, roto, Lada - roto, grasa, sol - alemanes, mayfren tabaco, mayfren, weraryufron, chica, chico. Un chulo vestío de Ed Hardy, chulo plateado. El horror estaba en la mente, la barbarie, gallina prieta árbol, sacrificio trapo rojo, puedo sentir el infierno en mi mente y en la mente de los otros, puedo sentir el infierno. Huevones sentados en los muros, pollos muertos en la bahía, restos de ratas, petróleo, reguetón, carros viejos, la mulatica linda, el yuma feo, la estampita, Cristo.

Las damas hacen juego a la derecha, la que no vaya presa no cobra!

Era placer en el cerebro y creía que era felicidad. Era placer y creía que era amor.

Como un planeta loco.

El carburador del carro en baja, en alta, en alta, mi organismo en alta, cuando el calzo del motor se rompe el acelerador cae en un vacío, "el vacío entra como el timbre en una casa", "como un despertador entra la muerte".

Línea buscando Malecón, huevones sentados en los muros, muro, cuando el calzo del motor se rompe.

16

The void enters like the doorbell at a house
—José Lezama Lima

Death enters like an alarm clock
—J. A. Baragaño

Havana, assholes sitting on the walls, assholes at street corners, the
vendor—cocky guy—gold grill in teeth, stench of piss in doorways, the
old Communist lady / the old Opposition lady, the narcissistic blogger,
the Communist cretin, the guy who could care less, flashy types. Chubby
Germans / slim mulatto girls, their eyes in my eyes, chubby Germans /
mulatto girls, a Lada model, a broken model, Lada-broken, grease, sun—
Germans, *myfren* tobacco, *myfren*, *wheraryufron*, girl, guy. Cocky guy
sports Ed Hardy, silver bling. The horror is in the mind, the incivility,
brown hen tree, sacrifice red rag, I can sense the hell in my mind and
in the minds of the others, I can sense the hell. Assholes sitting on the
walls, dead chickens in the bay, rat cadavers, petroleum, reggueton, old
cars, the pretty mulatta, the ugly American, little religious image, Christ.

The Ladies play to the right, if she doesn't get arrested she can't collect!

It was pleasure in the brain and I thought it was happiness. Pleasure,
and I thought it was love.

Like a crazed planet.

The carburetor of the car on low, on high, on high, my organism on
high, when the engine block breaks the accelerator falls into a void, "the
void enters like the doorbell at a house," "death enters like an alarm
clock."

Línea St. looking for the Malecón, assholes sitting on the walls, wall,
when the engine block breaks.

17

> Las hormigas trabajan por algo importante: comida.
> —Jack Spicer

Tenías que enfermar para que algo cambiara.

Mis dedos en la lata azul. Taxi Ford del 48.

Los políticos trabajan por cosas importantes,

las hormigas por comida, hacen hilera en la loza.

Tenías que enfermar, mis dedos en la lata azul,

basura en las esquinas, lineamientos.

Mis dedos en la lata azul, mis dedos en.

La dirección política de tu vida.

Los políticos trabajan por cosas importantes.

17

> Ants work for something important: food.
> —Jack Spicer

You had to get sick for something to change.

My fingers on the blue can. Taxi '48 Ford.

Politicians work for important things,

ants work for food and make a line across the tile.

You had to get sick, my fingers on the blue can,

garbage on the street corners, guidelines.

My fingers on the blue can, my fingers on.

The political direction of your life.

Politicians work for important things.

18

En la oscuridad vi las luces de la base naval. Recordé el avión de Barbados, *"eran sólo unas negritas"*. "Le conozco las entrañas". La perla conserva el dolor de la arena.

18

In the darkness I saw lights from the naval base. I remembered the bombing of Flight 455, *"They were only a few negresses."* "I know its entrails." The sand's sorrow is kept by the pearl.

19

El punto crítico de la bomba atómica emite luz azul. Cuando coges desinfectante en las manos se vuelve caliente. Hay una relación entre el alma y los cojones. La carretera, una línea blanca en la oscuridad, mi muerte, una línea blanca.

19

At its critical point the atomic bomb emits blue light. When you get disinfectant on your hands it feels hot. There's a relation between the soul and a man's balls. Highway, a white line in the darkness, my death, a white line.

20

Thought is a man in his wholeness wholly attending.
—D. H. Lawrence

En la meseta de la cocina, una hilera de hormigas, mi padre inclina la cabeza.
Es increíble la vida, me dice, yo veo su cerebro brillar. Conciencia, un ser atento.
Mi padre, un hombre en plenitud, totalmente iluminado.

20

> Thought is a man in his wholeness wholly attending.
> —D.H. Lawrence

On the kitchen countertop, a line of ants, my father leans his head over them.
Life is incredible, he says to me, I see his cerebrum flare. Awareness, an attentive presence.
My father, man in plenitude, utterly illuminated.

21

Qué estás pensando?
—Facebook

I

Yo pienso en todo ese humo contra los mosquitos, en todas esas cade-
nas de oro falso, en mi esqueleto en una caja allá en La Habana, en
todas esas rayas que dividen la calzada y pienso en el destino y en las
moscas que tropiezan contra el vidrio y en todos esos bancos de hospi-
tales bajo el alma y en mis padres que envejecen y en mis padres juntos
y pienso en el amor, sobre todo, siempre pienso en el amor, más que
nada, pienso en el amor, más allá de todo, siempre pienso en el amor
y pienso en gente llevando flores a los muertos y pienso en las flores y
en los muertos y en lagartos que se tragan a mosquitos y en mosquitos,
y pienso el Big Bang como acto de violencia y en el mundo como acto
de violencia y en los collares de la cobra* como un acto de violencia y
pienso en las almas gemelas, en estados que nos llevan hacia el miedo
y pienso en el miedo y el poder, sobre todo siempre pienso en el poder,
el punto azul de la bomba, el punto crítico. Y en el amor, sobre todo,
siempre pienso, en el amor.

*José Álvarez Baragaño

21

I
I think about the fumigation smoke for mosquitos, about all those
chains of fake gold, about my skeleton in a box there in Havana, about
all those stripes dividing the road surface and I think about fate and flies
that smash into the glass and about all those hospital benches below the
soul and about my parents getting older and about my parents together
and I think about love, more than anything, I'm always thinking about
love, above all else, I think about love, beyond all else, always thinking
about love and about people carrying flowers to the dead and I think
about flowers and about the dead and about lizards who swallow mos-
quitos and about mosquitos, and I think about the Big Bang as an act of
violence and the world as an act of violence and the coils of the cobra*
as an act of violence and I think about twinned souls, in states that
transport us toward fear and I think about fear and about power, more
than anything else I think about power, the blue point on the bomb, the
critical point. And about love, more than anything, I'm always thinking,
about love.

*José Álvarez Baragaño

22

Malecón, Habana, olas blancas, el mar rompiendo contra el muro, resaca, lo que el mar da, lo que devuelve, esponja, deuda, frente frío, los viejitos con sus huesos, frío, los viejitos en sus huesos, lo que el mar da, lo que devuelve.

22

Malecón, Havana, white waves, the ocean breaking against the wall,
undertow, what the ocean gives, what it returns, sponge, debt, cold front,
little old people with their bones, the little old people in their bones,
what the ocean gives, what it returns.

23

En la cola del banco, día de jubilados, un mar de viejos en un país viejo, se han quedado solos.

Este mar de viejos, ha hecho esta mierda, pienso, y se la comen, este mar de viejos ha hecho esta mierda y me la como, este mar de viejos ha hecho esta hazaña, las hormigas trabajan por algo.

En las colas de los jubilados, en las calles, hormigueros. Viejitos con ropas manchadas, círculos de grasa, ropa vieja.

23

In line at the bank: retiree day, an ocean of old people in an old country, they've been left on their own.

This ocean of old people, they created this shit, I think, and they eat it, this ocean of old people created this shit and I eat it, this ocean of old people did this great feat, ants work for something.

In the lines of retirees, in the streets, anthills. Old people with stained clothes, circles of grease, old clothes.

24

Comprendo la historia de un país en el expressway, Miami, viejitos raspando la loto. El día viene, una rosa metálica rosada. Bloqueo. Políticos como rock stars, una falsa muerte - un scrach en la pasta del disco, dentro del micro wave, la luz de un papel de plata.

24

I comprehend a nation's history on the expressway, Miami, old people scratching lotto cards. The day is coming, a pink metal rose. Embargo. Politicians like rock stars, a faked death—a scratch on the plastic of the disc, inside the microwave, light off a silver plate.

25

En el café, el hierro de las sillas al correrse.

Batidora triturando hielo.

So I felt all those butterflies, as people say,
butterflies in my stomach.
Vi que te brillaban los ojos, yo vi tus ojos brillar.
Sentí como brillaban los míos, como brillaban sentí.

25

In the café, the iron of chairs when they slide.

Blender grinding ice.

So I felt all those butterflies, as people say,
butterflies in my stomach.
I saw that your eyes were twinkling, saw your eyes twinkle.
I felt mine twinkling. As they twinkled, I could feel it.

26

Mi abuela usaba el Larousse para estudiar, se sentaba en la cama y escribía las palabras.

Leía en un susurro, después de la Revolución había llegado por fin al sexto grado.

Mi hermanito se metía en mi cama de noche, para protegerse del miedo.

Eran los 80, amábamos a los nicas y a Rambo. Jane Fonda, ponía de moda los aerobics.

Uno vuelve a la infancia como a un sueño, a la memoria como a un sueño, como a un sueño, uno vuelve.

26

My grandmother used the Larousse to study, she sat on her bed and
wrote out the words.
She read in a whisper, after the Revolution she had finally gotten to sixth
grade.
My little brother climbed into my bed at night to protect himself from
the fear.
It was the '80s, we loved Nicaraguans and Rambo. Jane Fonda popular-
ized aerobics.
One returns to childhood like a dream, returns to memory like a dream,
like a dream one returns.

27

Cuando toco mi cráneo es lo más cerca que llego,
lo más cerca de mi yo, que llego: la materia crea cosas a ella distintas.
En la calle, derrumbes, libretas de racionamiento, colas.
La posibilidad capitalista. El cambio político trae un cambio físico.

27

When I touch my skull that's the closest I get,
the closest to myself I can get: matter creates things other to itself.
Along the street, collapsing buildings, ration booklets, lines of people.
Capitalist possibility. Political change brings about physical change.

28

Uno tiene que vivir dispuesto a perder todo.

La muerte vuela como una tiñosa,
como una idea, sobre mi cabeza.

He visto cómo sale el aire de las gomas.
Cuando la palanca empuja, sale el aire como un alma.

28

To live, you have to be okay with losing everything.

Like a scabby bird, like an idea,
death wings over my head.

I've watched how air escapes tires.
When the lever is thrust, air hisses out like a soul.

29

I

Trajeron al vecino de Angola en una cajita, él, que andaba siempre en moto con side car. Una noche mató un carnero y fuimos a botar los restos en el campo, una bolsa tibia con estómago y con pelos. A la hora de comer comí su carne. Días después volví al lugar: la bolsa estaba rota, auras tiñosas, peste.

2

Huelga de hambre. Me levantaba en la mañana y mi padre decía, murió otro. La dama de hierro. Atravesábamos la línea del tren. Ahora va a salir un león entre las hierbas, yo le daba la mano confiado, quería que apareciera el león. Me levantaba en la mañana. Murió otro papá? La dama de hierro. Va a salir un león entre la hierba.

3

Baje por Prado y vi las luces que rodeaban el Ballet, una flecha dibujada en la calzada. El infierno tiene a veces una puerta de placer. El miedo sus círculos. Excarcelaciones, destierro, licencia extrapenal. Julio Antonio Mella. Bajé por Prado y vi las luces que rodeaban el Ballet. Un perro reventado en la calzada. Una era en descomposición. Gusanos. La carne muerta se hincha.

29

1

They brought our neighbor home from Angola in a little box. The one who always drove around on a motorcycle with a sidecar. One night he killed a ram and we went to the countryside to get rid of the remains, a warm sack with stomach and bits of fur. When it was time to eat, I ate its flesh. Days later I went back to the place: the sack was torn, scabby buzzards, stench.

2

Hunger strike. I would get up in the morning and my father would say, another one died. The Iron Lady. We'd cross the train tracks. Now a lion will appear amongst the grasses, I'd give it my hand, trusting, I wanted the lion to appear. I would get up in the morning. Would another daddy die? The Iron Lady. A lion will appear in the grass.

3

I walked down the Prado and saw lights all around the Ballet, an arrow sketched on the pavement. Sometimes a gate through pleasure leads to Hell. Its circles fear. Prison releases, exile, conditional leave. Julio Antonio Mella. I walked down the Prado and saw lights all around the Ballet. A dog, burst open on the pavement. An era of decomposition. Duffel bags. Dead flesh swells.

30

La cárcel, la enfermedad, la muerte. El amor, el éxito, la fama. Las cartas sobre la mesa.
Protegido por los muertos. Aun siento el latir del corazón de la paloma, veo sangre en el pico del gallo.

30

Jail, infirmity, death. Love, success, fame. Letters
on the table.
Safeguarded by the dead. I even hear the pigeon's heart beating,
glimpse blood on the rooster's beak.

31

Cambia el mundo si te beso, si te beso, cambia el mundo? En la radio del carro, botones antiguos. Temporada de pelota, Industriales–Santiago. Cambia el mundo si te beso, si te beso, cambia el mundo? Temporada de pelota, el sol de la carretera. Mi corazón y él: manchas.

31

Does the world change if I kiss you, if I kiss you does it change the world?
On the car radio, old buttons. Baseball season, the Industriales versus
Santiago. Does the world change if I kiss you, if I kiss you does the world
change? Baseball season, highway sun. My heart, and him: stains.

32

Un tipo que se llamaba Henjo escribió:
Te arranqué solamente porque tu nombre me extasiaba,
flor de Ominaeshi.
Envié eso a su teléfono solo para ver, la luz de la pantalla,
la luz de la pantalla, iluminando su rostro.

32

A guy called Henjo wrote:
I pulled you up only because your name entranced me,
Ominaeshi flower.
I sent that to her phone only to see light from its screen,
light from its screen illuminating her face.

33

Te besé solamente porque tu rostro me extasiaba,
flor de Ominaeshi.

33

I kissed you only because your face entranced me,
Ominaeshi flower.

34

El puntilleo constante del ser dentro de ti.
—Artaud

Un tanque de basura con humo, una moto que se enciende. Una bicicleta con letrero Marco Polo, en la radio, I want to know what love is. La niebla toca las flores como si no existiera. En Neptuno, un río de desempleados. La manera en que el terror funciona. El puntilleo constante del miedo dentro de ti, del amor dentro de ti. En la bodega estatal, un gato sobre la pesa de comprobación, un negocio privado, dos mundos que se encuentran, por primera vez, en mucho tiempo. Portales, calle Reina, suciedad del piso en mi cabeza, lozas partidas y mugrientas. Detrás de los cristales, héroes socialistas, flores plásticas. La niebla toca las flores como si no existiera. Un papel sucio flotando en la calzada, humo. En la radio, I want to know what love is.

34

A garbage bin spilling smoke, a motorcycle that catches fire. A bicycle
with a Marco Polo sign, on the radio *I want to know what love is*. Fog
grazes flowers as if it didn't exist. On Neptuno Street, a river of the
unemployed. The way in which terror functions. The constant stippling
of fear within you, of love within you. In the state-run corner store, a
cat on mechanical scales, a small private business, two worlds meeting
for the first time in a long while. Portales, Reina Street, the filth from
the floor in my head, tiles split and grimy. Behind the glass windows:
socialist heroes, plastic flowers. Fog grazes flowers as if it didn't exist. A
dirty paper floating across the road, smoke. On the radio *I want to know
what love is*.

35

No tienen ojos las fieras para lo bello. El ser como objeto. Para las ratas desde que nacen, el mundo es alcantarilla. No tiene ojos la bestia para lo bello. Desde que nace, se arrastra la serpiente. Los políticos quieren quórum. No tienen ojos para lo bello las fieras. Desde que nace, el objeto del ser, desde que nacen, los cobardes sienten miedo.

35

Brutes don't have eyes for beauty. Self as object. When rats are born, the sewer is their world. The beast doesn't have eyes for beauty. When the serpent is born, it slides across the ground. Politicians want a quorum. Brutes don't have eyes for beauty. The object of the self knows when it's born, when they're born, what cowards know is fear.

36

Siempre volvía a ti porque el amor. Tocaban rumba en La timba, el corazón de África.

Siempre volvía a ti porque el amor. Había pasado el momento.

36

I'd always return to you out of love. They played rumba in La Timba, heart of Africa.
I'd always return to you out of love. The moment was over.

37

I think of Dean Moriarty.
—Jack Kerouac, *On the Road*

2

Yo pienso en los cristales de la nieve y en paisajes de un milímetro de diámetro y en organismos de un milímetro de diámetro y en universos de un milímetro de diámetro y pienso en cosas que han vivido sin ser vistas y en la estructura de la célula y en las olas que se elevan sobre el muro y en pancartas con consignas socialistas y en moléculas de ADN y en los close-up de las películas del oeste y en el peso de la luz y en la onda de la luz y en la punta enrollada del helecho y en los días de Mercurio y en las lágrimas de las lámparas de araña y en nosotros convirtiéndonos en otros y en nosotros convirtiéndonos en otros y pienso en mitocondrias y electrones y el espacio y en colillas aplastadas contra el piso y en nosotros convirtiéndonos en otros y en nosotros convirtiéndonos en otros y en estrellas que miramos en pasado, la cara de Jackie Chan descascarándose en un bolso y en los tres mil de la luz en un segundo y en nosotros convirtiéndonos en otros y en nosotros convirtiéndonos en otros y en nosotros convirtiéndonos en otros y en nosotros convirtiéndonos en otros.

3

Yo pienso en el centro del sol y en el cable enrollado del teléfono y el formol de las manos de Guevara y en las raíces de los bosques y en los colores del lagarto y en tomografías de pulmón y en los dientes delanteros de las ratas y en nosotros convirtiéndonos en nada y en nosotros convirtiéndonos en nada y en nosotros convirtiéndonos en nadas y pienso en las rayas de la cebra y el boquear de los pescados en la tierra y en el bacilo de Koch y en el eureka y en nosotros convirtiéndonos en nada y en nosotros convirtiéndonos en nada y nosotros convirtiéndonos en nadas y pienso en el gas de Júpiter y en nosotros convirtiéndonos en otros y en nosotros convirtiéndonos en otros y pienso en el

37

I think of Dean Moriarty.
—Jack Kerouac, *On the Road*

2
I think about snow crystals and landscapes one millimeter in diameter and
about organisms one millimeter in diameter and universes one millimeter
in diameter and I think about things that have lived without ever being
seen and about the structure of the cell and about waves that break over the
wall and placards with socialist slogans and DNA molecules and close-ups
in westerns and about the weight of light and the waving of light and about
the curled tip of a fern and about days of Mercury and teardrop pendants
on spider lamps and about us transforming ourselves into other people
and about us transforming into others and I think about mitochondria and
electrons and space and cigarette butts crushed on the ground and about
us transforming ourselves into others and about us transforming ourselves
into others and about the stars that come into our sight out of the past,
Jackie Chan's face peeling off a duffel bag, and the three thousand per
second of light and about us transforming into others and us transform-
ing into others and us transforming into others and us transforming into
others.

3
I think about the center of the sun and the curled telephone cable
and the formaldehyde with Guevara's hands and about the roots of
the forests and about the lizard's colors and about lung scans and rat
incisors and about us transforming ourselves into nothing and us
transforming ourselves into nothing and us transforming ourselves
into nothingness and I think about stripes on zebras and the gasping
of fish on land and about tubercle bacillus and about the eureka and
about us transforming into nothing and about us transforming into
nothing and us transforming into nothingness and I think about the
gases of Jupiter and us transforming into others and us transforming

quantum y el enredo y en la noche que se extiende por los campos, el vacío que contiene la materia, el latido de mi tía en la pantalla y pienso en el núcleo del sol y pienso el centro del sol y en nosotros, convirtiéndonos, en otros.

4

Yo pienso en esos objetos en el suelo donde se trancan las varillas de las puertas y en la mancha de Gorbachov y en el verde de los paños de hospital y en el sentido de la lluvia y en la consciencia de la célula y en el azul de Urano y en los anillos de Urano y en las playas que se esconden en las perlas y en la electricidad de las neuronas, los relámpagos de nuestro cielo mental y pienso en las alas prietas de las gallinas prietas y en los quilos y en el óxido en la güira y pienso en Bosnia e Hiroshima y en Ruanda y en Bagdad y en Nagasaqui y en la electricidad de las neuronas y en las tormentas de nuestros cielos mentales.

5

Y pienso en la UMAP y en la revolución de cuando era un niño y en pioneros por el comunismo y en lo que ven los babalaos cuando empiezan a morirse y en patria o muerte venceremos, la luz de Sachsenhausen sobre hornos para infantes y pienso en arbeit macht frei y en las ondas de posibilidad y en las partículas de experiencia y en el campo unificado y en la liebre de los galgos y pienso en dios y en las carnadas. La coherencia entre la pudrición y la peste, entre la muerte y la peste, entre la descomposición y la muerte. Pienso en arbeit macht frei y en la muerte de Martí y en no me pongan en lo oscuro y en la muerte de Fidel y en a morir como un traidor y en la de Villena y Guiteras. Los ojos de Abel descansando sobre un plato y pienso en meteoritos y en neones y en apellidos terminados en kovsqui y en las células muertas de cuando yo era un niño y en los ojos de Abel descansando sobre un plato y en los ojos del Che tan abiertos en la muerte y pienso en arbeit macht frei y en Guantánamo y en las papilas de la lengua y en el sabor del hielo y en pistolas impresas y en los átomos de hidrógeno y en las cruces que se asoman en la vía. Yo pienso en arbeit mach frei y en Valeriano. En la sonrisa de Bush y Berluscony. Yo pienso en arbeit macht frei.

ourselves into others and I think about the quantum and entangle-
ment and about night that lengthens across country sides, the vacuum
that contains matter, my aunt's heartbeat on the screen and I think
about the sun's nucleus and I think the center of the sun and about
us, transforming, into others.

4

I think about those devices on the floor used for barring doors and about
Gorbachev's stain and about the green of hospital scrubs and about the
meaning of rain and the consciousness of cells and about the blue of
planet Uranus and the rings of Uranus and the beaches hidden inside
pearls and about the electricity in neurons, lightning across our mental
skies and I think about the brown wings of brown chickens and about
kilos and about coins rusting inside gourds and I think about Bosnia and
Hiroshima and Rwanda and Baghdad and about Nagasaki and electricity
in neurons and about the storms in our mental skies.

5

And I think about the camps run by Military Units to Aid Production
and about the revolution when I was a boy and about the child-pioneers
for Communism and speaking in unison and about what the baba-
lawos see when their death first approaches and about ¡Patria o Muerte!
¡Venceremos!, about the light of Sachsenhausen falling on ovens for
infants and I think about arbeit macht frei and about waves of possibil-
ity and about particles of experience and about unified field theory and
the hare for greyhound racing and I think about god and decoys. The
coherence of rot with pestilence, death with pestilence, decomposition
with death. I think about arbeit macht frei and about Martí's death and
about Don't leave me out in the dark and about Fidel's death and about
dying as a traitor and about the deaths of Villena and Guiteras. Abel's
eyes resting on a plate and I think about meteorites and neon lights and
about surnames ending in kovsky and about the dead cells from when
I was a boy and about Abel's eyes resting on a plate and about how very
open Che's eyes were in death and I think about arbeit macht frei and
about Guantanamo and about the tongue's taste buds and about the
flavor of ice and about the three-dimensional printing of guns and about
hydrogen atoms and crosses that appear along the way. I think about

6

Yo pienso en los objetos artificiales de las ciudades del futuro y en el
calor de los iglúes y en la piel de las termitas y pienso en la claridad y
en el lóbulo frontal y en la red de las neuronas y en el pasillo del onco-
lógico cuando cae la noche y en las glándulas de la oncóloga cuando
cae la noche y en la soberbia de la oncóloga cuando cae la noche y en
la perra de la oncóloga cuando cae la noche y pienso en la ambición y
en la búsqueda y en mi tía bajo la Vía Láctea y en marcelo bajo la Vía
Láctea y en mi muerte bajo la Vía Láctea y en nuestras muertes bajo la
Vía Láctea y en esos mundos en los que no voy a nacer, en los que no
voy a morir, en los que nunca has nacido, en los que nunca has muerto
y en los palillos dentales y en los bosques encerrados en los libros y en la
madera de las páginas en blanco y en la fosforescencia de las rosas en la
noche y en el amor de los perros y en las cosas que no sé de mí y en las
que voy a saber y en la voluntad del salmón y en el mundo de los recién
nacidos y en los ojos de los recién nacidos y en la lógica del cardumen
y en mi tía bajo la Vía Láctea y en mi muerte bajo la Vía Láctea y en las
especies extintas y el trabajo del bufón y la actitud de los bufones y en
los hombres bombas y en las bombas y en lo que ven los poetas cuando
empiezan a morirse, y lo que ven los poetas cuando entran al círculo y
en lo que ven las personas cuando empiezan a morirse.

7

La curva del malecón a 140, la flor que me señaló mi tía el día antes,
la inteligencia de mi padre, la primera vez que vi a mi hermano. El día
que lloré por Cristo. El día en que conocí a Cristo. El Peugeot blanco de
mi infancia. La luz de los corales fluorescentes, las flores de Julia en el
balcón. El cura del barrio judío en la iglesia de Roma. El contra cielo en
una hoja impresa. Los días del amor, la mañana en la frontera.

8

La fuerza de los brazos mecánicos, las gotas de los sueros, la brillantez
de la lluvia, las flores biseladas del espejo. La impresión de las sombras
en las paredes de Nagasaqui. Las piedras falsas en las mezclillas de las
gentes, la consciencia política, el socialismo de estado, la inquisición. Los
juguetes plásticos, la muñeca sin brazos, las gotas en el frío del cristal, las
encrucijadas de los pueblos. El polvo de los camiones. El reguetón en la

arbeit macht frei and about Valeriano. About Bush's smile, and Berlusconi's. I think about arbeit macht frei.

6

I think about artificial objects in cities of the future and about the warmth of igloos and about termite skin and I think about clarity and the frontal lobe and about the neuron network and the hallways in the oncological hospital at nightfall and about the oncologist's glands as night is falling and about the oncologist's arrogance as night is falling and the bitchiness of the oncologist as night is falling and I think about ambition and the search and about my aunt under the Milky Way and about marcelo under the Milky Way and about my death under the Milky Way and about our deaths under the Milky Way and about those worlds in which I will never be born, in which I will never die, about worlds where you have never been born, in which you've never died and about toothpicks and the forests enclosed in books and about the wood of blank white pages and the way roses phosphoresce at night and about love between dogs and about the things I don't know about myself and about the things I will know about myself and about the salmon's fortitude and about the world of newborns and the eyes of newborns and about the logic of schools of fish and about my aunt under the Milky Way and my death under the Milky Way and about extinct species and the fool's job and the fool's attitude and about suicide bombers and about the bombs and about what poets see when they begin to die, and what poets see when they enter the circle and about what people see when they begin to die.

7

The Malecón's curve at 140 kph, the flower shown to me the day before by my aunt, my father's intelligence, the first time I saw my brother. The day I cried for Christ. The day I came to know Christ. The white Peugeot from my childhood. Light from fluorescent coral, Julia's flowers on the balcony. The priest from the Jewish barrio in the Roman church. *Le contre-ciel* on a printed page. Days of love, morning at the border.

8

The strength of mechanical arms, drops of mitomycin solution, brightness of the rain, beveled flowers in the mirror. The impressions of

playa, los tatuajes de presidio. El mar, las pelotas que flotan como perlas.
Las huellas de grasa en el garaje. Las palabras de Hatuey cuando iba hacia
la hoguera. El cisne de yeso en el estante, las flores que cayeron en la
iglesia.

9
Explicar la poesía al tubo de la quimio de la tía, a la bolsa de quimio de la
tía, a la gota de la quimio. El puntilleo constante. Un gorrión vuela sobre
mi cabeza, un hombre lee, en una cara del tenis tiene un semicírculo
rojo que completa un sol en el piso pulido, algunas cosas tienen que
morir, otras, desaparecer, la idea de la poesía a una rata muerta, o mejor,
la idea de la poesía de una rata muerta, en una rata muerta. A la manilla
del reloj kichón decir: si la energía de tu vida no pasa por tu mano a la
escritura. Explicar la poesía a una rata muerta.

10
Y pienso en la OTAN y en el grupo de los siete y en Pinochet y en Sen-
dero Luminoso y en lo blanco del anón, lo verde del anón, lo negro del
anón y en la cortina de hierro y en el mundo como objeto y en la muerte
como objeto y en el aire del esófago y en el amor de los ciegos y en el
encendedor de cocina cuando salta la chispa y en la muerte bajo la Vía
Láctea y en mi muerte bajo la Vía Láctea y en la rotación de la tierra, pero
sobre todo pienso en ti, sobre todo pienso en ti, yo pienso mucho, en ti.
Yo estoy pensando siempre en ti, yo pienso siempre, en ti.

shadow on walls at Nagasaki. The fake jewels people wear on denim, political consciousness, state socialism, inquisition. The plastic toys, the doll without arms from that poem, drops on the cold glass, town crossroads. Dust from trucks. Regguetón on the beach, prison tattoos. The sea, balls that float like pearls. Greasemarks in the garage. Hatuey's words as he moved toward the bonfire. The plaster swan on the bookshelf, flowers that fell down in the church.

9
Explain poetry to my aunt's chemo tube, to my aunt's chemo bag, to the chemo drops. A constant stippling. A swallow flies over my head, a man reads, a face on a sneaker includes a red semicircle that forms a complete sun against the polished floor, some things have to die, others must disappear, the idea of poetry to a dead rat, or better yet a dead rat's idea of poetry, on a dead rat. Say to the secondhand on your überkitschy watch: whether your life force does not pass through your hand into the writing. Explain poetry to a dead rat.

10
And I think about NATO and about the G7 and about Pinochet and about the Shining Path and about the whiteness of the sugar apple, the greenness of the sugar apple, the blackness of the sugar apple and about the iron curtain and about the world as object and about death as object and about air in the esophagus and about love for the blind and about the kitchen lighter when it sparks and about death under the Milky Way and about my death under the Milky Way and about the earth's rotation, but most of all I think about you, most of all I think about you, I think about you, a lot. I'm always thinking about you, I always think, about you.

38

A medida que avanza el día, en el balcón, se iluminan las orquídeas.

38

As day moves across the balcony, the orchids light up.

39

Puedo sentir el sol en sus mejillas.

39

I can sense sun on their cheeks.

40

Flotaba el astro rojo sobre el mar. Algunas cosas tienen que morir, otras, desaparecer.

40

The red comet floated across the sea. Some things have to die. Others must disappear.

41

Las gotas en el parabrisas corrían hacia abajo. Yo estaba solo.

41

Drops on the windshield were sliding downward. I was alone.

42

Et j'ai vu quelquefois ce que l'homme a cru voir!
—Rimbaud

Al borde de los sueños a veces te susurran al oído, en el borde del camino, a veces, he oído lo que el hombre creyó oír, en las encrucijadas de los pueblos, el viento trae polvo. A veces se hace un círculo de hojas. Estoy acercándome al círculo, peligrosamente al círculo. La claridad. Lo raro es lo normal.

42

Et j'ai vu quelquefois ce que l'homme a cru voir!
—Rimbaud

At the edge of dream they sometimes whisper in your ear, at the edge
of the road, sometimes, I've heard what the man thought he heard, at
crossroads in the towns, wind brings dust. Sometimes there's a circle
of leaves. I'm getting closer to the circle, dangerously close. Clarity.
Strangeness is the norm.

43

Despertar y ver que había muerto,
un pañuelo en su cabeza,
bajo la Vía Láctea.

43

Waking up to see that she died,
a kerchief on her head,
under the Milky Way.

44

1

Salí de la ciudad y me tumbé en el campo, flotaba la tierra, la Vía Láctea, de noche no podía ver la lluvia. Su descenso.

2

En la fonda, al borde del camino, un chulo registraba el bolso de una puta, en una serie de televisión, un borracho decía: mis ojos eran dos cobras líquidas. Recordé: cuando El Buda iba a iluminarse fue cuando más fuerte atacó el demonio; dudo que exista tal cosa, si existe, debe de ser gradual, el círculo mágico, la vacuidad resplandeciente, es un lugar a donde entras, pero de donde debes salir. Después del infarto, le dijeron al vecino, no te duermas, que ese sueño que sientes, es la muerte.

44

1
I left the city and lay down in the countryside, the earth was floating,
Milky Way, at night I couldn't see the rain. Its descent.

2
In the cantina, by the roadside, a pimp was searching a whore's hand-
bag, on a TV series, a drunk was saying: my eyes were two fluid cobras.
I remembered: the moment when the Buddha was about to be enlight-
ened came when the demon attacked most viciously; I doubt that any
such thing exists, if it exists, it must come gradually, the magic circle,
the resplendent emptiness, it's a place you enter, but you have to get
out. After the heart attack they told the neighbor, don't sleep because the
dream you're sensing is death.

45

Choco de frente con el sentido, con la fuerza del viento en la calzada. La ciudad se llena de turistas, de casas reparadas y burgueses, de electrones corriendo por los cables. De niño, la luna iba junto al carro, yo estaba siempre atrás, todo corría. Ahora voy delante. En un poema, un tipo que iba a prisión la atrapaba y se la metía en la boca como un ácido, o era la pupila de un lobo? La pila de un reloj en la lengua, como un ácido, o es la pupila de un lobo? New restaurants, pescados en sartenes, el brillo de las súper novas, las luces de los carros a lo lejos, los polos opuestos donde salta el destello. Decirle al pescado en la sartén, el arte no debe de ser inocuo, el arte debe traspasar el arte. Los mundos son sólo acerca del ser. Un Haiku: la forma en que el musgo se ilumina. Pero la poesía no es, la poesía en verdad no es nada. Estar despierto todo el tiempo, revelar lo que la muerte revela.

45

Suddenly I collide with meaning, with the wind's force on the road. The city fills with tourists, with fixed-up bourgeois homes, electrons rushing through the lines. When I was a child the moon moved alongside the car, I was always in the back, everything rushed past. Now I sit up front. In a poem, a guy on his way to prison trapped the moon on his tongue, like LSD, or was it the pupil of a wolf's eye? The watch battery on your tongue, like LSD, or is it the pupil in a wolf's eye? *New restaurants*, fish in frypans, the sparkle of supernovas, headlights from very far away, the spark jumping between opposed poles. Tell the fish in the pan, art should not be innocuous, art should perforate art. Worlds are only about the self. A haiku: form in which moss catches light. But poetry does not exist, poetry really isn't anything. Be awake continuously, reveal what death reveals.

46

Una vez en el poder la intimidación funciona sola (paranoia) cámaras de vigilancia. Hay cosas que crecieron a mi lado, cosas que murieron a mi lado. Cuando el viento aparece en la calzada, la hierba se dobla.

46

Once in power intimidation is self-propelled (paranoia), surveillance cameras. There are things that grew next to me, things that died next to me. When wind picks up over the road, the grass bows.

47

Centro Habana, el vendedor en la quincalla, calor, Neptuno, la mercadería bajo un paño verde.
Yo iba a comprar con cien años de poesía encima, con mil años de contrabando, él.
Fijé la vista en el dorso de su mano, las costillas de su perro hablaban del amor, fijé la vista en el dorso de mi mano, las líneas de la palma hablaban de un amor, escrito.

47

Central Havana, the salesman at a stand, heat, Neptuno St., merchandise hidden under a green cloth.
I would go out shopping with a hundred years of poetry weighing me down, a thousand years of contraband, him.
I focused on the back of his hand, his dog's ribs spoke of love, I focused on the back of my hand, the lines on my palm spoke of love, a love written down.

48

1

El futuro llegó y está vacío. La ciudad, propaganda - metamorfosis, publicidad barata. Los cactus viven con poco, protegen sus frutos con espinas. En la barbería pensar el corte de Kim Jong-Un. En la playa pensar: La perla devuelve a la arena la solidez de la roca. Una silla plástica, el plástico cuando es nuevo brilla, cuando es viejo, es feo. En la radio, canciones mediocres, discursos mediocres, una realidad mediocre. Un supuesto socialismo, una mentalidad feudal del poder. A veces el cielo en la noche se enciende y se refleja en el cristal de la mesa. A veces caen dos flores del balcón al mismo tiempo, vicarias.

2

En la playa un tipo baila rumba frente a un Yuma. Frente al agua, una tiñosa come desperdicios, brujería, un cuerpo mojado de gallina. La convicción de la gente en la magia. Algunos pinos sueltan resina cuando son cortados. Después de soltar la tinta, en los calamares, un cristal adentro. Un vendedor de uvas criollas (ácidas). Una mujer con un vestido en el mar, un cangrejo blanco en la arena. El horizonte de sucesos dobla el tiempo, dicen. Espantar al aura y decir al cuerpo de gallina: En la vida, una verdad sin adorno. No es país para poetas. Una silla plástica en la arena. Al poder, decir: estás lleno de existencia.

Olas, un mundo líquido al que llaman tierra.

48

1

The future arrived and it is empty. City, advertising—metamorphosis,
cheap publicity. Cacti live on very little, protecting their fruits with
thorns. Think in the barbershop about Kim Jong-Un's haircut. Think
on the beach: The pearl returns the stone's solidity to the sand. A plastic
seat, when plastic is new it gleams, when it's old, it's ugly. On the radio
mediocre songs, mediocre speeches, a mediocre reality. A putative socia-
lism, a feudal mentality of power. Sometimes the night sky lights up and
is reflected on the glass tabletop. Sometimes two flowers fall from the
balcony at the same time, stand-ins.

2

At the beach a guy dances rumba in front of a North American. By the
water a turkey vulture eats remains, ritual, the wet body of a hen. The
people's belief in magic. Some pines leak sap when they're cut. After
some squid release ink, a glassy center. Someone selling local grapes
(acidic). A woman in the ocean in a dress, a white crab on the sand. The
horizon of events bends time, they say. Startle the aura and say to the
hen's body: An unadorned truth in life. It's no country for poets. A plas-
tic chair on the sand. Say to power: you are full of existence.

Waves, a liquid world they call earth.

49

Riego las matas, la expresión vegetal de lo que busco, me dices, los americanos de la playa se creen un modelo de sociedad bonito. En las calles, en La Habana, reyecitos criollos. Si hay algo que no peligra en la vida es lo mediocre. Si hay algo que fascina al poder, es lo mediocre.

49

I water the plants, the vegetal expression of whatever I'm trying to find, you say, the Americans on the beach imagine they're an attractive model for society. In the streets, in Havana, our little criollo kings. If there's anything that's not endangered in life, it's mediocrity. If there's anything that fascinates power, it's mediocrity.

50

En el cine, atravesó la luz del proyector, como un fantasma atravesando otro. Sentí el tiempo, la idea del horizonte, como la niebla, no hay un punto en donde empiezan, donde termina un punto. Estar adentro de una nube, en el cine atravesó la luz.

***

De niño vivía fascinado por las constelaciones. La Osa Mayor, la menor. Las buscaba sin encontrarlas en el cielo. De adulto las busco. Cuando veo una no veo la otra. Me creía destinado a estar contigo. Cuando veo una, no veo la otra.

***

Jugábamos al tío vivo, corría alrededor para impulsarlo, luego me subía tratando de alcanzar el centro, así también después lo hice en la vida, me impulsaba tratando de crear. De niño, cuando lo lograba, me quedaba en el centro por instantes, hasta que el mundo, dejaba de dar vueltas.

50

In the cinema, she passed through the light from the projector, like one ghost passing through another. I felt time, the idea of the horizon, like fog, there's no one place where they begin, no one point where they come to an end. To be inside a cloud, in the cinema, she passed through the light.

***

As a child I spent my time fascinated by constellations. Ursa Major, Ursa Minor. I'd try to find them in the sky but I couldn't. As an adult I try to find them. When I see one, I don't see the other. I thought I was destined to be with you. When I see one, I don't see the other.

***

We'd go on the merry-go-round, we ran in circles pushing it to make it move, then I'd try to jump all the way to the middle, just as I later did in life, I tried to make myself move in order to create. As a child, when I did it, I'd stay there in the middle for seconds until the world stopped spinning.

51

Fin de año, puedo ver las almas de los puercos sobre la ciudad, son unas cosas trasparentes. Un policía se persigna cruzando la calle, dos flores de majagua giran con el aire. La democracia es el himno de la derecha. El de la izquierda, la igualdad. Banderas americanas en las tendederas, un viejo sin camisa, un ruso con cigarros amarillos.

51

Year's end, I can see pig souls above the city, they're transparent objects.
A policeman crosses himself as he walks across the street, two hibiscus
flowers spin with the breeze. Democracy is the hymn sung by the right.
Hymn sung by the left: equality. US flags on clotheslines, an old man
with no shirt, a Russian with yellow cigarettes.

52

En la televisión del bar, un documental sobre el cosmos: Explotan al morir enviando energía en todas direcciones, supernovas. Muchas estrellas orbitan entre sí. En cinco mil millones de años el sol se convertirá en una gigante roja. Le debes la vida a una estrella. Afuera lo real, revolución o barbarie, proletariado y burguesía. En las cafeterías privadas las puticas del campo. Los newbanricans, los chulitos de La Habana. Las películas tratan del amor, las canciones hablan del amor. La vida sin amor da miedo. Las ideas viajan más lejos que la luz, (Fidel Castro) la luna no pesa, flota, atrae las mareas, una ola y luego otra y luego otra. En la barra dos calvos sacan cuentas frente a frente, salgo a la ciudad, me meto la mano en el bolsillo y recuerdo:

*He caminado largos años por las congeladas calles de La Habana y jamás he visto el alma, más bien, un hormigueo constante, he atravesado largos años y jamás he visto al líder, más bien voz de televisores, el enjambre sube y baja por las calles, por la historia. He caminado por las calles de la historia y jamás he visto nada, más bien héroes en las paredes, más bien héroes en los enjambres.

La política es de los alfas. La fama. Saco la mano del bolsillo, calderilla, menudos, uno tiene la cara del Che, el otro no.

He andado largo tiempo por los helados campos de Ostergotland. Jamás he visto un alma.
—Tomas Transtromer

52

On television at the bar, a documentary about the cosmos: supernovas, they explode when they die, sending energy in all directions. Many stars orbit each other. In five billion years the sun will become a red giant. You owe your life to a star. Outside, the real, revolution or barbarism, proletariat and bourgeoisie. In private cafes, the too-young whores from the countryside. The Cubeau-riche, Havana's pimps. Movies are about love, songs talk about love. Life without love leads to fear. Ideas travel farther than light (Fidel Castro), the moon weighs nothing, it floats, attracts the tides, a wave and then another and another. On each side of the bar two bald guys add up tabs, head to head. I go out into the city, I put my hand in my pocket and remember:

*For long years I've walked through Havana's frozen streets and have never seen a soul, instead I saw a constant uneasiness, I've walked for years without ever seeing the Leader, instead I heard the voice from televisions, the swarm marches up and down the streets, through history. I've walked the streets of history and never saw anything, instead I saw heroes on the walls, heroes in swarms instead.

Politicking is for the alphas. Fame. I take my hand out of my pocket, small change, trivialities, one has the face of El Che, the next one does not.

> For a long time I've walked through the frozen fields of Östergötland. I've
> never seen a soul.
> —Tomas Transtromer

53

Yo me acuerdo de Adalberto que peleó con El Che y bajó de las lomas y murió de cirrosis sin haber bebido nunca. Me acuerdo de la corona plateada de sus dientes y de su corazón y de su alma. Yo me acuerdo de Adalberto que bajó de las lomas con El Che y fue policía y chofer y zapatero remendón. *El bichito siempre me engañó*, decía refiriéndose a Fidel. El día de su muerte, no fui a verlo en su ataúd, estaba cansado y llovía. Yo me acuerdo de Adalberto, recuerdo su corazón y su alma y su sonrisa y la corona plateada de sus dientes de nácar.

53

I remember Adalberto who fought with El Che and came down from the hills and died of cirrhosis without ever drinking. I remember the silvery crowns on his teeth and his heart and his soul. I remember Adalberto who came down from the hills with El Che and was a police officer and a driver and a cobbler. *The little brat always fooled me*, he said, referring to Fidel. On the day he died, I didn't go to see him in his shroud, I was tired and it was raining. I remember Adalberto, I remember his heart and soul and smile and the silver crowns on his pearly teeth.

54

En Neptuno, los carros de alquiler. Zapata y 12, la boca del cementerio. Si lo que te define es el miedo. El mundo como ser, el mundo como objeto. Tu cuerpo como ser tu cuerpo como. Incluso cuando tu cuerpo es sólo objeto, el mundo es todo ser.

Como la obra, desde el feto, al final, transformaciones. Un gato que parece un tigre. El mundo no tiene trascendencia, una mota de algodón sin peso, un perro que parece un lobo. La mediocridad más grande, no es una obra mediocre, sino una vida sin amor. El ojo blanco de la noche flota otra vez, con la liebre adentro.

Derrumbes, árboles sobre ruinas, las raíces buscan en el vacío una tierra que no existe, asfalto.

54

On Neptuno St., rental cars. Zapata and 12th, the mouth of the cemetery. If the thing that defines you is fear. The world as presence, the world as object. Your body as presence your body as. Even when your body is just an object, the world is all presence.

Like the work, from fetus to finale, transformations. A cat resembling a tiger. The world has no transcendence, a weightless puff of cotton, a dog resembling a wolf. The greatest of all mediocrity is not a mediocre work but a loveless life. The night's white eye floats again, the hare inside it.

Collapsed buildings, trees on ruins, roots in the void seeking some non-existent earth, asphalt.

55

Me desperté pensando en la muerte, en cosas como entrar al mundo es entrar al ser, me desperté pensando en finales. En el balcón, el bonsái decidió echar flores, se había quedado sin hojas y decidió echar flores.

Me desperté pensando en la muerte, en cosas como salir del mundo es salir del ser, me desperté pensando en finales. En el balcón, el bonsái decidió echar flores, se había quedado sin hojas y decidió echar flores.

55

I woke up thinking about death, about things like how entering the world is entering presence, I woke up thinking about endings. On the balcony the bonsai decided to burst into flower, it lost its leaves and decided to burst into flower.

I woke up thinking about death, about things like how departing the world is departing one's presence, I woke up thinking about endings. On the balcony the bonsai decided to burst into flower, it lost its leaves and decided to burst into flower.

56

La política norteamericana del embargo ha fracasado
—Barack Hussein Obama

El día después del discurso, miré la silla y me dije: Van a levantar el bloqueo. En el supermercado recordé un poema. Un tipo se identificaba con Hamlet frente a un pomo de aceitunas, cabezas flotando en salmuera, el cráneo de Yorick en mi mano, cabezas que flotan en el pomo. El bloqueo era lo más sólido que tenía la realidad. Fidel era lo más sólido. En Santa Ifigenia, un buldócer remueve la tierra, construyen una tumba. La tumba de Fidel.

56

The policy of the embargo has failed
—Barack Hussein Obama

The day after the speech, I looked at my chair and said to myself: They're
going to lift the embargo. In the supermarket I remembered a poem.
A guy who identified with Hamlet in front of a bottle of olives, heads
floating in brine, Yorick's skull in my hand, heads floating in a bottle.
The embargo was the most concrete aspect of reality. Fidel was the most
concrete. In Santa Ifigenia a bulldozer removes earth, they're building a
tomb. Fidel's tomb.

57

Puse un pomo de agua en el congelador. El hielo al expandirse quebró el vidrio. El craquear de un cristal. Los borrachitos de Galiano dormitan sobre el churre. Santa Claus, disfraces, en los bares, gente cool, gente linda. Javana, una fruta con escarcha de la guerra fría. Luces de carros. Puse el pomo en el fregadero. El cristal con el agua fue cayendo poco a poco. El mundo no es un objeto, es un ser y estoy vivo.

57

I put a bottle of water in the freezer. When the ice expanded, it broke the glass. The cracking of a crystal. The drunks on Galiano nap on their layers of grease. Santa Claus, masks, in bars, cool people, beautiful people. Aaaahhbana, a frozen fruit from the Cold War. Headlights. I put the bottle in the sink. The glass and water dripped out a little at a time. The world is not an object, it's a presence and I'm alive.

Language Notes

This is the first publication of the complete Spanish-language original work, as well as the first translation of the book into English. Marcelo Morales opted to blend Cubanisms of the moment into the original version of *El mundo como ser*, writing "in Habanero," in Havana Spanish. As a result some details of his original Spanish are deliberate but might look like errors, even to other Spanish-language readers. Examples of written words evoking pronunciations characteristic of Havana street life: *vestío*, instead of *vestido*; *meao* instead of *meado*; *dienté oro* instead of *diente de oro*. In a specific twist on the "local" nature of the Spanish, Morales tempered some uses of Cuban vernacular. After he gave a reading in Uruguay in early 2015, Morales took out the verb *coger*. In much of Latin America, this flexible verb is associated with sex in a way that he was not invoking within the Cuban context, where the intention is less edgy—ex. it can simply mean "to grab." Morales decided that the contrast within Spanish-language cultures was distracting and replaced the Cuban variant. Kristin Dykstra opted to keep street names in Spanish. In addition to recognizing a common practice in cultural commentaries about Cuba, we prefer the sound of "Línea," the name of Morales's own street, to "Line."

As we remark in the introduction and detailed notes, Morales incorporates bits of English into his original. In earlier versions of the translation, we experimented with reversal, embedding Spanish into the English rendition. However, we ultimately opted to recognize that languages circulate in different ways in the contemporary world. Spanish signifies differently in English-language societies than does English within contemporary Cuba. As translator Vera Kutzinzki wrote of her own brilliant rendition of Nicolás Guillén's *The Daily Daily*, the "practice of linguistic subversion is exceedingly difficult to reproduce in English, especially since English is one of the languages being subverted" (xxiii). Dykstra therefore echoes Morales's English but places it in italics as an "other" English.

Notes on the Poems

Prompted by the translation of this work into English, the author collaborated with the translator to write the following notes. We identify references that might not be immediately clear to readers unfamiliar with aspects of life in Havana past and present, and we note particular associations that the author finds important.

I

The Ladies: Short for the Ladies in White (Las Damas de Blanco). The Ladies are a dissident organization created by women whose families include political prisoners. In years leading up to the composition of this book, they received relatively consistent media attention outside Cuba, especially in the Miami area, and they have been a familiar reference point within Havana. However, Morales specifies that at the time he was composing his book, the Ladies didn't seem to have a clear platform in terms of a political future they would imagine or propose for Cuba; this was not really their purpose. For him the Ladies represent a kind of limbo: they are a political reference, yet one through which the speaker senses an inability to identify with any political party or its visions for a future, since there seems to be a lack of developed options.

6

Machado: Gerardo Machado y Morales [1871–1939]. Cuban dictator defeated in the 1933 Revolution.

9

The donkey and the abyss: both refer to "Rapsodia para el mulo" (Rhapsody for the mule), a famous poem by José Lezama Lima. It opens, "Surefootedly, indeed, the mule steps into the abyss," and Lezama spins variations on this image throughout his poem. (English translation by G.J. Racz from *José Lezama Lima: Selections*, ed. and int. Ernesto Livón Grosman. Berkeley and Los Angeles: U of CA Press, 2005.)

10

Response Brigades (Brigadas de respuesta): Sometimes denoted in English-language publications as RRBs, their full names are "Rapid

Response Brigades." These are groups of civilians controlled by the government, which are used (sometimes in violent ways) to repress protests that the government classifies as counter-revolutionary.

The Malecón: An iconic structure in Havana that features in many famous photographs and paintings, the Malecón is a road along the sea. Cars, which reappear throughout these poems due in part to Morales's occasional work driving visitors in a Soviet-era Lada, move in relatively large numbers down the Malecón, in comparison to some of the closed or more damaged streets throughout Havana. The name of the Malecón also conjures the presence of people and architectural majesties. That is, the Malecón exists also through its famous seawall, which runs along the road and marks the line where the city encounters the sea. Residents gather alongside and on top of the wall for informal socializing in the space it creates between the buildings, the cars, and the ocean.

Línea Street: Another cue on this page that contributes to mapping the speaker's location within the very large and sprawling city of greater Havana. Línea runs through the Vedado neighborhood.

II

Mahh-racas: North American tourism was reduced substantially and deliberately by the Cuban government after 1959 as a step away from neocolonialism, one of many platforms to create a new society. The resurgence of dependence on tourism after 1989 is one of the marked and controversial signs of change in recent decades. Morales includes some English phrases within the otherwise Spanish-dominant flow of the book in order to signify the ways in which English is heard in Havana in the twenty-first century: in the streets, from visitors as well as locals attempting to engage them. The connotations are rich yet can shift from example to example, in terms of their suggestions about differences of perspective. Here *"the Cuban mahh-racas, the Cuban artist. The Cubans"* hints at how a resident walking down the street can not only become part of the stage set of tourism—which constantly produces imagery of Cubans and "Cuban culture" for outsiders—but hear and understand enough English to comprehend how that process is happening. Italics appear in the English translation to highlight the coexistence of more than one kind of English.

16

myfren, wheraryufron: This adaptation from the English "My friend, where are you from?" references the way that some Cubans have learned phrases in other languages—here English—in order to engage visitors to their city. With the spelling of the phrase Morales suggests speech with an accent.

17

"Lineamientos" is a term used by Raúl Castro's administration in documents about the reorganization of politics and economy in Cuba. Political observers have translated this term into English as "guidelines," so here the translator follows suit.

18

"They were only a few negresses": Dismissive statement famously attributed to Orlando Bosch, long thought to have orchestrated the bombing of Cubana Aviation's Flight 455 along with exile Luis Posada Carriles. The bombing took place on October 6, 1976, near Barbados. It is understood as an act of violent opposition to the Castro government. However, since this act was directed against an airplane full of diverse travelers, any focused political justification of the act is weakened, and the racism manifest in the quotation has a similar weakening effect. Readers of English are often curious about the murky histories of opposition and conspiracy animating the US–Cuba divide—including events that took place before many of today's readers were even born. Some may therefore be interested in looking through the declassified documents about this incident posted at the National Security Archive (hosted by George Washington University), which involve both the US and Cuba. The archives demonstrate that within one day of the bombing, an FBI office in Venezuela received information naming both Bosch and Posada; the two had worked with a team to execute the bombing of Flight 455, and they were eventually prosecuted in Venezuela. However, as a 2006 report at the Archive summarizes, "Posada escaped from prison in September 1985; Bosch was released in 1987 and returned to the United States illegally. Like Posada, he was detained by immigration authorities; over the objections of the Justice Department, which determined he was a threat to public security, the first President Bush's White House issued him an

administrative pardon in 1990" (http://nsarchive.gwu.edu/NSAEBB/NSAEBB202/index.htm 8 April 2015). In the political contestations between Cuba and the US that marked the late twentieth century, this controversial public pardon made it possible for Cuba to claim that the US hosted a terrorist—a claim that the US was also making against Cuba.

I know its entrails (Le conozco las entrañas): an allusion to a phrase by José Martí. After a prolonged stay in the late nineteenth century in United States as a political exile, seeking collaboration amongst his fellow "Americans" in the hemispheric sense, Martí's enthusiasm for his northern neighbor became tempered. He witnessed the rise of openly expansionist ambitions and feared that US designs on Cuba might compromise his island's independence. Martí referred to the US as a monster or beast, sometimes evoking its great size but also suggesting a warning. Morales refers to Martí's statement, "I lived inside the monster and I know its entrails" ("Viví en el monstruo y le conozco las entrañas").

27

Collapsing buildings (derrumbes): Buildings around Havana suffered a lack of repair during years of economic crisis that followed the international changes symbolized by 1989 and the fall of the Berlin Wall. In Havana, these collapses became a key symbol of uncertainty about the effects of political realignments. Similarly, with a resurgence of tourism and corresponding surge in photography of Havana circulating worldwide, Havana's ruins became powerful symbols abroad. In the Old City of Havana, a designated historic sector, the Office of the City Historian has carried out a series of building renovations; symbolically, that office tried to respond to assumptions that the collapsed buildings necessarily signify the collapse of the island's society and government in a post-Soviet era. More recently, other approaches to renovation have begun to emerge out of the limited private sector, enabled by the government's new Guidelines (Lineamientos).

Ration booklets (Libretas de racionamiento): for many years in Cuba, the ration booklet was the central point of access to food subsidized by the state. The abundance or lack of this food has been tied to the country's economy. Morales notes that in the past 25 years, the number of products available through the ration booklet has been meager. Some Cubans can access additional food in other ways, while others cannot. He specifies that elderly Cubans who live alone often have difficulty obtaining food through other means.

29

1

Angola: During Morales's childhood, Cuba took part in war in Angola, which left him with memories about the impact of wars in far-off lands. Among the Cubans who died in Angola were parents of friends and other people he knew. Morales also recalls the symbolic power of Angola within the Cold War context. Not only were Angolans, Namibians, and South Africans part of the war, but also the Soviet Union and the United States. He recalls the year 1989, when Cuban forces defeated the South African army, pushing it out of Namibia. South Africa's practice of apartheid gave this event extra meaning, because it enhanced the public argument that Cubans were helping to liberate an oppressed state. Morales adds, "In my childhood, Cuba functioned as a miniature Socialist power. It was part of the idea of a proletarian internationalism." Cuba sent troops to many nations, including Nicaragua (named elsewhere in this book), El Salvador, Ethiopia, and more.

3

Julio Antonio Mella [1903–1929]: Cuban politician, student leader, founder of Cuba's Communist Party. He is known, among other things, for the hunger strike he launched to protest his incarceration by the dictator Gerardo Machado.

37

2

This poem extends the series begun in poem 21.

3

The formaldehyde with Guevara´s hands (el formol de las manos de Guevara): After the execution of revolutionary leader Ernesto "Che" Guevara [1928–1967] in Bolivia, his hands were cut off and sent to an Argentine laboratory for fingerprint identification. The hands were put into a bottle of formaldehyde. Later the amputated hands disappeared, and stories differ as to their fate.

5

Military Units to Aid Production (Unidades Militares de Ayuda a la Pro-
ducción): Commonly known by the acronym, as "las UMAP." These units
functioned like forced labor camps, to which people were sent if they were
considered scourges on society at that time. Most often this designation
was given to the religious and to homosexuals, particularly men, the major-
ity of whom were seen as the negation of the "New Man" mythologized by
the revolution to guide and symbolize social reforms. UMAP camps were
active from 1965 to 1968. Morales's reference to the UMAPs might be
understood as a gesture toward a broader conversation within the island.
That is, Cuba's society and government have now openly admitted prob-
lems with the way the UMAP camps were used in the 1960s, as carefully
phrased in this 2010 statement from Fidel Castro to the *Los Angeles Times*
about taking "responsibility" for injustice: http://latimesblogs.latimes.
com/laplaza/2010/09/castro-interview-gay-persecution.html.

Babalawos: sometimes spelled *babalaos,* this term refers to priests
dedicated to Ifá, part of the ecology of Afro-Cuban religious practices that
have come to be influential across racial lines on the island. Morales asks
what they see; the *babalaos'* vision can have both individual and com-
munity effects. The priests perform divination ceremonies and issue an
annual letter about the year, among other activities. Their work is tied to
a vision of history. Religious studies scholar Stephan Palmié puts it this
way: "Suffice it to note that the supreme oracle, *Ifá,* is not just a corpus of
divinatory verses and techniques, but a personal being (known as *Orun-
mila*) who was witness to the creation of the world. [. . .] *Ifá,* we might
say, is the supreme historian—priests specifically dedicated to his cult
(*babalaos*) often speak of *ifá* as the ultimate book" (*Wizards & Scientists:
Explorations in Afro-Cuban Modernity and Tradition,* Durham: Duke UP,
2002; 297n15).

Rubén Martínez Villena [1899–1934]: Cuban politician and writer. In
August 1933, he was one of the principal Communist leaders in a general
strike that became a key event in the path toward defeating the dictator
Machado. One year later he died in Havana.

Antonio Guiteras Holmes [1906–1935]: Cuban politician born in the
United States. Guiteras was a prominent fighter against the Machado

dictatorship. After Machado's fall, he participated in the 100-Day rule through the ministry of governance. Holding strong anti-imperialist sentiments, Guiteras took measures that impacted the interests of the US government and the Cuban oligarchy, such as promoting the eight-hour workday and an intervention in Cuba's electrical company. Morales sees a famous document later written in prison by Fidel Castro, "History Will Absolve Me," as having many points in common with Guiteras's platforms and ideas.

Abel's eyes resting on a plate / Los ojos de Abel descansando sobre un plato: Abel Santamaría was the second in command in the movement that assaulted the Moncada Barracks on July 26, 1953, a major step on the path toward the Cuban Revolution of 1959. To carry out the psychological torture of Abel's sister, Haydée Santamaría, who was herself imprisoned in cells at Moncada, her captors presented her with a plate containing two eyes and told her they belonged to her brother.

Valeriano: Spain's General Valeriano Weyler [1838–1930]. Infamous amongst Cubans as a genocidal politician, Weyler was named Governor of Cuba in 1896, where he became the creator of concentration camps on the island. Morales recalls estimates that between 300,000 and 400,000 Cubans died in the camps during the war for independence from Spanish rule. Some commentators have tried to distinguish Weyler's "re-concentration camps" from other concentration camps of the twentieth century, arguing that his intention was to separate civilians from rebels as a military strategy, one that was somewhat successful. However, Weyler failed to provide anything resembling adequate provisions or safe living conditions for the relocated people, leading to mass disease and starvation; and his strategy further backfired in the political realm, because it gave opposition politicians grounds for publicizing and denouncing his treatment of Cuban civilians. Emphasizing the dehumanizing and horrific experiences created by Weyler's camps rather than the limited scope of his military intention, many people find it legitimate to compare his results to the conditions of infamous concentration camps from the twentieth century.

8

Regguetón: a musical genre popular in Cuba. Rap, hip-hop, and regguetón, which are all forms actively traveling through the Caribbean and

US, have engendered mixed responses in recent years. Some examples of these musical forms in Cuba are considered lively and exciting contributions to music: popular songs have the potential to blend local realities and cultural statements into larger conversations about social issues and empowerment, along with delivering musical innovation and excellence. However, the international commercial power of these forms has created an equal amount of concern, often focused on questions such as whether the importation and recirculation of such highly commercialized songs involves producing saleable art for international commercial settings and not for Cubans—e.g., questions about catering to the demands of dominant marketing circuits, thus losing sight of authentic and/or incisive cultural engagements on the island. There are also commonly voiced concerns about negative and divisive messages delivered through popular music and affiliated products, which are seen to promote an obsession with money and the display of status symbols: clothing brands, jewelry, commercialized rather than more organic interpretations of street identity, etc.

Hatuey's words as he moved toward the bonfire (las palabras de Hatuey cuando iba hacia la hoguera): Hatuey is one of the great historical figures whose image still holds in Cuban and Spanish literatures. An Arawak/Taíno cacique, or chieftain who arrived in Cuba from the island of Quisqueya (later Hispaniola, now divided into Haiti and the Dominican Republic), Hatuey warned local indigenous peoples about the evil that Spaniards would bring to them, and he offered to help them fight Spanish forces. He was captured and condemned to be burned at the stake in 1511. A famous retelling by Father Bartolomé de las Casas, one of the most famous of Spanish authors due to his denunciations of violence against indigenous peoples during the Conquest, appears in *The Devastation of the Indies*. It depicts Hatuey's last words as he was led to the stake. A Franciscan friar asked him if he wanted to convert to Christianity and go to heaven. Morales remembers the famous response. "For Hatuey, it was very simple," he recalls. "He didn't want to go live with the people who burned him alive. I don't want to be where such cruel people live, he said." Readers of English can see more in *The Cuba Reader*, an anthology from Duke University Press which includes a translation by Herma Briffault excerpted from *The Devastation of the Indies*, as well as short scholarly observations emphasizing the importance of Hatuey's legacy of resistance. Las Casas wrote that Hatuey "was told what he could do in the brief time that remained to him, in order to be saved and go to Heaven. The cacique, who had never heard any of this before, and was told he would go to Inferno, where, if he did not adopt the Christian Faith, he would suffer eternal torment, asked the Franciscan friar if Christians all went to Heaven. When told that they did he said he would prefer to go to Hell" (13).

48
2

Foreigner (Yuma): The translation of this term is interesting because of a slippage in meaning over time. Contemporary authors differ in their emphases. The term is sometimes used as a reference to tourists from the United States. Canadians have also been prominent in Cuban tourism in recent decades, and other contemporary writers have talked with Kristin Dykstra about their sense that usage of the term "Yuma" gradually widened to incorporate the influx of European and even Latin American tourists. Perhaps its usage differs depending on location and the sort of tourists a given place tends to attract. Here, Morales clarified that he is specifically thinking of North American tourists.

49
Criollo: this term links back to the Spanish colonization of the Americas. In the Spanish system, social and political orders took birthplace into consideration. It was most prestigious to be born as a peninsular Spaniard. "Criollo" was the term for a child born in the Americas to peninsular Spaniards. This was a step down in the overall Spanish hierarchy, but "criollo" still connoted a relatively European appearance and social role (in contrast to people long placed further down the social ladder, associated with mixed or primarily indigenous or African heritage). Over time uses of these identity labels would grow more complex, and sometimes the word "criollo" is used in a loose regional sense, as when it refers to a food or product from Latin America. However, "criollo" in Spanish does not translate nicely into "Creole," a word which connotes mixing in a different way in English. "Criollo" can retain its link to a Euroamerican appearance, and with it, a history of greater access to social and political power. These connotations are relevant to Morales's critique of "little

criollo kings," for the image ties into his critiques of power. His phrase is a critique of behavior: a presumptuous tendency to order other people around.

52

The Cubeau-riche (Los newbanricans): Neologisms. Morales made up "newbanricans" as a term rhyming and playing om words like "nouveau," "Cuban" and "ricos" (rich people). These are people who flaunt their emergent wealth, which was appearing on the island as government guidelines went into effect permitting partial privatization. The English translation, then, is a play on "Nouveau riche," a loan phrase in English from the French.

56

In December 2014, Presidents Barack Obama and Raúl Castro issued highly publicized partner statements regarding their intentions to bring the embargo of Cuba to an end, and to reduce the political tensions between their nations. Many general listeners on both sides received the statements as a done deal: the embargo was over! However, the governmental statements did not represent a change *already* made to the vast network of laws and interests, both small and large, long institutionalized around the structures of US/Cuba opposition. Therefore, the announcements provoked explosions of simultaneous celebration, outrage, and hope—all leading to intense curiosity about what exactly would change, when it would change, and how change would take place in future years.

In 1989, Martin Majoor designed a groundbreaking serif typeface, FF Scala, for the Vredenburg Music Center in Utrecht. In 1991, FontFont released the face as FF Scala. It appears in this book, along with its sans serif version for titles.